LAW SCHOOL ESSAYS THAT MADE A DIFFERENCE

LAW SCHOOL
ESSAYS THAT MADE A
DIFFERENCE

Eric Owens
and The Staff of The Princeton Review

Random House, Inc.
New York
www.PrincetonReview.com

Princeton Review Publishing, L. L. C.
2315 Broadway
New York, NY 10024
E-mail: bookeditor@review.com

ISBN 0-375-76345-7

Editorial Director: Robert Franek
Editor: Erik Olson
Designer: Scott Harris
Production Editor: Julieanna Lambert
Production Coordinator: Scott Harris

Manufactured in the United States of America.

9 8 7 6 5 4 3 2 1

ACKNOWLEDGMENTS

Special thanks to Ian Van Tuyl, Rob Tallia, and David Adam Hollander, Esq., from whose solid foundation grew my own understanding of the law school application process.

Bob Spruill deserves plaudits for honing his LSAT test prep expertise into the fine section of Games strategy found at the back of this book.

I would also like to thank my editor, Erik Olson, for his counsel during my work on the manuscript.

CONTENTS

INTRODUCTION

HOW TO USE THIS BOOK

It's pretty self-explanatory.

The first part—you are reading it now—is about how to write a great personal statement for admission to law school. We think our advice is fairly indispensable. It's no magic bullet, of course, nor does it rise to the level of sophistication of, say, brain surgery. Nevertheless, if you follow our advice about what to put in and what to leave out, we're very confident that you'll end up with a memorable personal statement that will both differentiate you from the pack and make you tremendously competitive.

Just in case you won't take our word for it, the second part of this book is what the deans and directors of admissions at five of the most selective law schools in the nation had to say on the role that personal statements play in their admissions processes. We think you'll find intriguing the nuances of opinion on certain issues; they help to put a human face on the admissions process, which at times, as you'll find out shortly, can seem anything but human.

The third part of this book contains several actual, unexpurgated personal statements written by actual law school applicants to a variety of selective law schools. We think they're all solid. Some are excellent. More important, they've all passed the ultimate test for law school application greatness: their authors got accepted into at least one of the top law schools to which they applied.

These applicants wrote on a variety of topics, ranging from their relationships with family members to experiences in the working world to physical disabilities from which they suffer and how they continue to overcome them on a daily basis. There are statements with sad themes and others with more upbeat attitudes. Here you'll find stories of achievement and of failure.

It's also important to note that the statements you'll find in these pages were written by students of diverse backgrounds and for a wide variety of schools. And like most collections of prose by many different authors, these essays display a range of creativity and cleverness with the written word. Some are so good that they will intimidate you; others will make you say to yourself, "Hey, I could write something like that." Some are so strange and unexpected that you will wonder how one or some of the most selective law schools in the country accepted the people who wrote them.

Ideally, these personal statements will provide you with inspiration, narrative and organizational structures, themes, illustrious words and phrases, and ways to express yourself that you hadn't thought of and that help you communicate exactly what you want to communicate.

And we don't just tell you where each student got in, but in most cases also where they *didn't*. The point of doing so is to help you start to gain a better idea of the relative selectivity of each of these top law schools.

Because you may be just beginning the law school admissions process, we've included a bonus section of our LSAT test-taking strategies at the end of the book. We're confident that our advice in this realm is the finest around, and that if you invest the time to learn our approach, that investment will pay hefty dividends on the day of your test.

Finally, though it goes without saying: Don't plagiarize the personal statements in this book. That's worth repeating: Do not plagiarize the statements you read in this book. Different law schools ask different questions. Some simply ask for a personal statement. Others want you to answer several short essay questions in addition to writing a personal statement. Requested lengths will vary. We encourage you to note buzzwords, structures, and themes that you like. But draw the line at copying paragraphs, sentences, or even phrases. There's a chance you'll get busted, which would mean you couldn't get into law school at all. Plus, plagiarism is wrong, so you'd feel all icky inside. Why bother?

LAW SCHOOL ADMISSIONS: A BRIEF OVERVIEW

> "Genius is 1 percent inspiration and 99 percent perspiration."
>
> *—Thomas Edison,*
> *American inventor and holder*
> *of nearly 1,100 patents*

Law school admissions counselors will tell you until they are blue in the face that they do not use a formula when determining which applicants to accept and which to reject. Insofar as nobody will plug all the parts of your application into a mathematical equation that churns out yes's and no's, it's true that there is no formula.

In the grand scheme of things, though, getting into law school comes down to a very basic formula. Wherever you apply, your application will be divided into three roughly equal parts: (1) your undergraduate grades (and your graduate school grades, if you have any); (2) your LSAT score; and (3) "the subjective stuff," which is your personal statement, your professional experience, and all the other intangibles that can't be measured numerically. It is this third part that keeps the law school admissions process from becoming a closed, quantitative assessment.

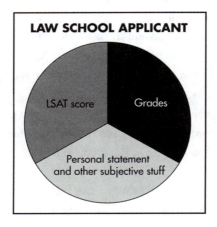

THE ADMISSIONS INDEX

When evaluating your application, law schools will usually combine your grades and your LSAT score into an "index." It's a number (which varies from school to school) that is made up of a weighted combination of your UGPA (undergraduate grade point average) multiplied by your LSAT score. Sadly but truly, your LSAT score is often weighted more heavily than your GPA.

Chances are that you are at a point in life where your UGPA is pretty much fixed (if you're reading this early in your college career, start getting very good grades pronto).

While the process differs from school to school, it is generally the case that your index will put you into one of three piles:

(Probably) Accepted. A select few applicants with high LSAT scores and stellar GPAs are admitted pretty much automatically. If your index is very, very strong compared to the school's median or target number, you're as good as in.

(Probably) Rejected. If your index is very weak compared to the school's median or target number, you are probably going to be rejected without much ado. When admissions officers look at weaker applications, they'll be looking for something so outstanding or unique that it makes them willing to take a chance (like, oh, just for example, *a truly incredible personal statement*). Other factors that might help here include ethnic background, where you are from, or very impressive work or life experience.

Well . . . maybe. The majority of applicants fall in the middle; their index number is right around the median or target index number. Folks in this category have decent enough LSAT scores and GPAs for the school, just not high enough for automatic admission. Why do most people fall into this category? Because people apply to schools they think they have at least a shot of getting into based on their grades and LSAT scores. This phenomenon is called self-selection. Harvard, for example, probably doesn't see very many applicants who got a 140 on the LSAT. What will determine the fate of those whose applications hang in the balance? One thing law schools often look at is the competitiveness of your undergraduate program. Someone with a 3.3 GPA in an easy major from a school where everybody graduates with a 3.3 or higher will face an uphill battle. On the other hand, someone with the same GPA in a difficult major from a school that has a reputation for being stingy with As is in better shape. Admissions officers will also pore over your personal statement, your letters of recommendation, and your resume for reasons to admit you, reject you, or put you on their waiting list.

Nonquantitative factors are particularly important at law schools that receive applications from thousands of numerically qualified applicants. "Top Ten" law schools that receive ten or fifteen applications for every spot in their first-year classes have no choice but to "look beyond the numbers." These schools will almost surely have to turn away hundreds of applicants with near-perfect LSAT scores and college grades; the subjective stuff of applicants who get past the initial cut will be scrutinized.

Less competitive schools are just as concerned, in their own way, with "human criteria" as are the Harvards and Stanfords of the world. They are on the lookout for capable people who have relatively unimpressive GPAs and LSAT scores. The importance of the application is greatly magnified for these students, who must demonstrate their probable success in law school in other ways.

THE LAW SCHOOL APPLICATION PROCESS: A CRASH COURSE

It's time-consuming and it's not too much fun. The LSAT alone can easily consume eighty or more hours of prep time, and a single application form might take as long as thirty hours if you take great care with the essay questions (as you should). You don't want to sabotage your efforts through last-minute sloppiness or let this already annoying process become a gigantic burden. Our advice: Start early and pace yourself.

Georgetown University

"You may write your personal statement on any subject of importance to you that you feel will assist us in our decision."

WHEN TO APPLY

If you apply to Stanford, your application must be postmarked no earlier than September 1 and no later than February 1. The deadline at Boston College is March 1, but the folks in admissions "urge you to submit your application well before the March 1 deadline." At the University of Tennessee, applications received before February 15 will be afforded something called "priority consideration," while applications received February 15 will be considered late and may not be reviewed at all. At Loyola University Chicago School of Law, you must have your application entirely completed by April 30.

The longer you wait to apply to a school, regardless of its deadline, the worse your chances of getting into that school may be. No efficient admissions staff is going to wait for all the applications before starting to make their selections. If you're reading this in December and hope to get into a law school for the fall but haven't done anything about it, you're in big trouble. If you've got an LSAT score you are happy with, you're in less trouble. Your applications, however, will get to the law schools after the optimum time and may appear a bit rushed. The best way to think about applying is to start early in the year, methodically take care of one thing at a time, and *finish by December.*

Early admissions options. Many schools have early admissions options, so you may know by the holiday season if you've been accepted. Naturally, early admissions means early application. For example, early admissions applicants at Duke University School of Law must have taken the LSAT no later than June and all application materials must be received no later than November 1.

Early admission is a good idea for a few reasons. It can give you an indication of what your chances are at other schools. It can relieve the stress of waiting until April (or June or August) to see where you'll be spending the next three years of your life. Also, it's better to get waitlisted in December than April (or whenever you would be notified for regular admission); if there is a "tie" among applicants on the waiting list, they'll probably admit whoever applied first. Of course, not every school's early admissions option is the same. Some schools don't even have one.

Rolling admissions. Many law schools evaluate applications and notify applicants of admission decisions continuously over the course of several months (ordinarily from late fall to midsummer). Obviously, if you apply to one of these schools, it is vital that you apply as early as possible because there will be more places available at the beginning of the process.

Applying Online

Most law schools allow applicants to submit applications via the Internet. While typing is not exactly rocket science, it is a pain in the neck. A few services can make the process easier. The LSACD, an online service (215-968-1001 or www.lsac.org; $54), has a searchable database and applications to all 185 ABA-approved schools.

THE BIG HURDLES IN THE APPLICATION PROCESS

Take the LSAT. The Law School Admission Test is a roughly three-and-a-half-hour multiple-choice test. The LSAT is given in February, June, October (or, occasionally, late September), and December. It's divided into five multiple-choice sections and one (almost completely useless) writing sample. All ABA-approved and most non-ABA-approved law schools in the United States and Canada require an LSAT score from each and every applicant.

Register for LSDAS. You can register for the Law School Data Assembly Service at the same time you register to take the LSAT; all necessary forms are contained in the *LSAT/LSDAS Registration Information Book* (hence the name). You can also register online at www.lsac.org.

Complete applications from six or seven schools. Fairly early—like in July—select a couple "reach" schools, a couple schools to which you've got a good shot at being accepted, and a couple "safety" schools where you are virtually assured of acceptance. Your safety schools—if you were being realistic—will probably accept you pretty quickly. It may take a while to get a final decision from the other schools, but you won't be totally panicked because you'll know your safety school is there for you. If, for whatever reason, your grades or LSAT score are extremely low, you should apply to several safety schools.

Arizona State University

"[A] personal statement, written by you, and no longer than three double-spaced typed pages, is required as part of the application. In this statement we seek information about you. Statements about law in general or law and society will not be useful. The statement should provide information about your distinctive qualities, talents, successes, achievements and life experiences."

Write your personal statement. Many, many schools will simply say, in one variation or another, "Tell us about yourself." However, it's critical that you personalize every essay for each individual law school to which you apply. Also, some schools will ask you to write a few shorter essays in addition to your primary personal statement—one more reason you need to select your schools fairly early.

Obtain two or three recommendations. Some schools will ask for two recommendations, both of which must be academic. Others want more than two recommendations and want at least one to be from someone who knows you outside traditional academic circles. As part of your LSDAS file, the Law School Admissions Council (LSAC) will accept up to three letters of recommendation on your behalf and will send them to all the schools to which you apply. This is one of the few redeeming qualities of the LSDAS. The last thing the writers of your recommendations are going to want to do is sign, package, and send copies of their letters all over the continent.

Update/create your resume. Most law school applications ask that you submit a resume. Make sure yours is up-to-date and suitable for submission to an academic institution. Put your academic credentials and experience first—no matter what they are and no matter how much professional experience you have. The resume is just a supplement to the rest of the material; it's probably the simplest part of the application process.

Get your academic transcripts sent to LSDAS. When you subscribe to Law School Data Assembly Service, you must request that the registrar at every undergraduate, graduate, and professional school you ever attended send an official transcript to the LSDAS. Don't even think about sending your own transcripts anywhere; these people don't trust you any farther than they can throw you. *Make these requests in August.* If you're applying for early decision, start sending for transcripts as early as May. Law schools require complete files before making their decisions, and LSDAS won't send your information to the law schools without your transcripts. Undergraduate institutions can and will screw up and delay the transcript process—even when you go there personally and pay them to provide your records. Give yourself some time to fix problems should they arise.

Write any necessary addenda. An addendum is a brief letter written to explain or support a deficient portion of your application. If your personal and academic life has been fairly smooth, you won't need to include any addenda with your application. If, however, you were ever on academic probation, arrested, or if you have a low grade point average, you may need to write one. Other legitimate addenda topics are a low/discrepant LSAT score, DUI/DWI suspensions, or any time gap in your academic or professional career.

Send in your seat deposit. Once you are accepted at a particular school, that school will ask you to send some cash its way. A typical fee runs $250 or more. This amount will be credited to your first-term tuition once you actually register for classes.

Do any other stuff. You may find that there are other steps you must take during the law school application process. You may request a fee waiver, for example. Make extra-special-sure to get a copy of the LSAC's *LSAT/LSDAS Registration and Information Book*, which is unquestionably the most useful tool in applying to law school. It has the forms you'll need, a sample LSAT, admissions information, the current Law Forum schedule, and sample application schedules. You can find everything you'll need at www.lsac.org.

WRITING A GREAT PERSONAL STATEMENT

The personal statement often represents your only opportunity to differentiate yourself from the pack and to show that you can string more than a few sentences together. Sure, there's an essay on the LSAT, but it won't be taken anywhere nearly as seriously as your personal statement. Besides your grades and your LSAT score, your personal statement is the most important part of your law school application. Your answer should be about two or three pages long, and it should amount to something significantly more profound than "A six-figure salary really appeals to me" or "Things were going swell until I got canned by Arthur Andersen."

Willamette University

"The personal statement is a very important part of your application. Your statement will help us learn more about you, your professional aspirations and your reasons for applying to the graduate program. Please write an essay in response to the questions which follow, and feel free to provide additional information you would like the admission committee to consider in reviewing your academic record, professional experiences or personal accomplishments. Please limit the length of your personal statement to no more than three pages.

What are your career goals?

What experiences and influences significantly shaped who you are today?

How will this program contribute to your professional development?"

Be specific to each school. You'll probably need to write only one basic personal statement, but you must make absolutely sure to spin this one basic personal statement into a personal statement that is unique (even if it's only ever-so-slightly unique) to each law school to which you apply. Law school admissions officers see a number of essays that have been written for some school other than theirs, and they just hate that. Don't send the personal statement you wrote for your Fordham application to the University of Michigan. Pay super-close attention to what each school is asking for in the prompt for *its* personal statement because there are probably some subtle differences. Track each personal statement to make sure it goes to the right place.

> Whenever possible, go ahead and spring the extra $1.10 for the really fancy thick paper. Live a little.

THE ESSENTIALS

In your personal statement, you want to present yourself as intelligent, professional, mature, and persuasive. These are the qualities law schools seek in applicants. Moreover, these are the qualities that make good lawyers. Consequently, unlike in your application to college, the personal statement on a law school application is not the time to discuss what your trip to Europe meant to you, describe your wacky chemistry teacher, or try your hand at verse. While you want to stand out, you definitely don't want to be *overly* creative. And while you must differentiate yourself, you don't want to come across as a weirdo or a loose cannon. It's also usually important that you show why you want to go to law school.

Like any good writing, your law school application should be clear, concise, candid, structurally sound, and 100 percent grammatically accurate.

Clarity and conciseness are usually the products of a lot of reading, rereading, and rewriting. Without question, repeated critical revision by yourself and by others is the surest way to trim, tune, and improve your prose.

> Cut out excessive verbiage and wasteful words. Eschew obfuscation.

Candor is the product of proper motivation. Honesty, sincerity, and authenticity cannot be superimposed after the fact; your writing must be candid from the outset. Also, let's be on the level: you're probably pretty smart and pretty sophisticated. You could probably fake candor if absolutely necessary. But you shouldn't. For one thing, it's a hell of a lot more work. Moreover, no matter how good your insincere personal statement may be, we're brazenly confident that an honest and authentic personal statement will be even better.

Structural soundness is the product of a well-crafted outline. It really pays to sketch out the general themes of your personal statement first; worry about filling in the particulars later. Pay particularly close attention to the structure of your personal statement and to the fundamental message it communicates. Make sure you have a well-conceived narrative. Your personal statement should flow from beginning to end. Use paragraphs properly and make sure the paragraphs are in a logical order. The sentences within each paragraph should be complete and in logical order.

Gimmicks

Do not make your personal statement into a poem or an epic or anything besides standard prose. It never works.

Grammatical accuracy is a must. A thoughtful essay that offers true insight will stand out unmistakably, but if it is riddled with poor grammar and misspelled words, it will not receive serious consideration. *It is critical that you avoid all grammatical errors.* We just can't stress this enough. You aren't allowed to misspell anything. You aren't allowed to use awkwardly constructed sentences or run-on sentences. You aren't allowed to use verbs in the wrong tenses. You aren't allowed to misplace modifiers. You aren't allowed to make a single error in punctuation.

Don't neglect your spelling and grammar check. We imagine you'll probably write your personal statement on a computer. It's a very good idea. Use a computer with a spell checker. Turn on the spell- and grammar-checking options. Your computer is only as smart as you are, so carefully consider the advice your computer offers.

GRAMMATICAL CATEGORY	WHAT'S THE RULE?	BAD GRAMMAR	GOOD GRAMMAR
MISPLACED MODIFIER	A word or phrase that describes something should go right next to the thing it modifies.	1. Eaten in Mediterranean countries for centuries, **northern Europeans** viewed the tomato with suspicion. 2. A **former greens keeper** now about to become the Masters champion, **tears** welled up in my eyes as I hit my last miraculous shot.	1. Eaten in Mediterranean countries for centuries, **the tomato** was viewed with suspicion by northern Europeans. 2. **I was a former greens keeper** who was now about to become the Masters champion; **tears** welled up in my eyes as I hit my last miraculous shot.
PRONOUNS	A pronoun must refer unambiguously to a noun and it must agree (singular or plural) with that noun.	1. Though **brokers** are not permitted to know executive access **codes, they** are widely known. 2. The **golden retriever** is one of the smartest breeds of dogs but **they** often **have** trouble writing **personal statements** for law school admission. 3. Unfortunately, both **candidates** for whom I worked sabotaged their own **campaigns** by taking **a contribution** from illegal **sources**.	1. Though **brokers** are not permitted to know executive access **codes, the codes** are widely known. 2. The **golden retriever** is one of the smartest breeds of dogs but **it** often **has** trouble writing **a personal statement** for law school admission. 3. Unfortunately, both **candidates** for whom I worked sabotaged their own **campaigns** by taking **contributions** from illegal **sources**.
SUBJECT/VERB AGREEMENT	The subject must always agree with the verb. Make sure you don't forget what the subject of a sentence is, and don't use the object of a preposition as the subject.	1. **Each** of the men involved in the extensive renovations **were** engineers. 2. Federally imposed **restrictions** on the ability to use certain information **has** made life difficult for Martha Stewart.	1. **Each** of the men involved in the extensive renovations **was** an engineer. 2. Federally imposed **restrictions** on the ability to use certain information **have** made life difficult for Martha Stewart.
PARALLEL CONSTRUCTION	Words in lists in the same sentence need to be similar in form to the other words in the list.	1. The two main goals of the Eisenhower presidency were a **reduction** of taxes and **to increase** military strength. 2. **To provide a child** with the skills necessary for survival in modern life is **like guaranteeing their** success.	1. The two main goals of the Eisenhower presidency were **to reduce** taxes and **to increase** military strength. 2. **Providing children** with the skills necessary for survival in modern life is **like guaranteeing their** success.
COMPARISONS	You can only compare things to exactly the same things.	1. The **rules** of written English are more stringent than **spoken English**. 2. The **considerations** that led many colleges to impose admissions quotas in the last few decades **are similar to the quotas** imposed in the recent past by large businesses.	1. The **rules** of written English are more stringent than **those of spoken English**. 2. The **considerations** that led many colleges to impose admissions quotas in the last few decades **are similar to those** that led large businesses to impose quotas in the recent past.
PASSIVE/ ACTIVE VOICE	Choose the active voice, in which the subject performs the action.	1. **The ball was hit by the bat**. 2. After months **were spent** trying to keep justdillpickles.com afloat single-handedly, **resignation was chosen by me**.	1. **The bat hit the ball**. 2. After **I spent months** trying to keep justdillpickles.com afloat single-handedly, **I chose to resign**.

A Man of Diverse Talents

Sir Winston Churchill wasn't just a great prime minister; he was also a prolific writer and ultimately a Nobel laureate in literature. Once, when Churchill was reviewing the edited version of one of his many books, he noticed a sentence that a well-meaning editor had rewritten so that it would not end with a preposition. The story goes that Churchill wrote disdainfully in the margin, "This is the sort of bloody nonsense up with which I will not put."

Howard University School of Law

"Your personal statement assists the Admissions Committee in selecting a diverse entering class of students. It is also used to assess each applicant's written English skills. The personal statement provides applicants with an opportunity to describe the uniqueness of his or her character, abilities, and experience and to assist us in getting to know and understand you as a person. You should discuss those aspects of your background, experience, talents, achievements, and interests that you believe would be important for us to know. Applicants are encouraged to write about issues of diversity, academic history, community service activities, and professional experience. Personal statements should also detail the applicant's interest in Howard's Law School and how attending Howard will allow you to realize your dreams and aspirations. Your personal statement should be typed, double-spaced, and no longer than three pages. Your statement must be submitted with the application."

Good writing is writing that is easily understood. You want to get your point across, not bury it in words. Don't talk in circles. Your prose should be clear and direct. If an admissions officer has to struggle to figure out what you are trying to say, you'll be in trouble. Also, legal writing courses make up a significant part of most law school curriculums; if you can show that you have good writing skills, you have a serious edge.

Harvard University

"Because people and their experiences are diverse, you are the best person to determine the content of your own statement. It is for you to decide what information you would like to convey, and the best way for you to convey it. Whatever you write about, readers will be seeking to get a sense of you as a person and as a potential student and graduate of Harvard Law School. In this context, it is generally more helpful to write what you think readers should know to have a better sense of who you are rather than writing what you think the readers want to read."

Get to the point in three pages unless there are unusual circumstances. Don't be long-winded and boring. Admissions officers don't like long personal statements. Would you if you were in their shoes? Most people who have unusual circumstances are folks who are in their thirties or forties (or fifties or sixties) who have more life experience. Whatever your story, get to the point. Be brief. Be focused.

Buy and read *The Elements of Style,* by William Strunk, Jr. and E. B. White. We can't recommend it highly enough. In fact, we're surprised you don't have it already. This little book is a required investment for any writer (and believe us, you'll be doing plenty of writing as a law student and a practicing attorney). You will refer to it forever, and if you do what it says, your writing will definitely improve.

Have three or four people read your personal statement and critique it. Proofread your personal statement from beginning to end, then proofread it again, then proofread it some more. Read it aloud. Keep in mind, though, that the more time you spend with a piece of your own writing, the less likely you are to spot any errors. You get tunnel vision. Ask friends, boyfriends, girlfriends, professors, brothers, sisters—anybody—to read your essay and comment on it. Have friends read it. Have an English teacher read it. Have an English major read it. Have the most grammatically anal person you know read it. Hire an editor if you feel it is necessary. We don't care. Just do whatever it takes to make sure your personal statement is clear, concise, candid, structurally sound, and 100 percent grammatically accurate.

New York University

"Because people and their interests vary, we will leave the content and length of your statement to your discretion. You may wish to complete or clarify your responses to items on the application form, bring to our attention additional information you feel should be considered, describe important or unusual aspects of yourself not otherwise apparent in your application, or tell us what led you to apply to NYU Law."

ADVANCED PERSONAL STATEMENT THEORY

A solid, well-crafted essay will impress any admissions officer, but if it looks like all the others, you will not be remembered. Yours will be just another personal statement, and as a consequence, you will present yourself as just another applicant. This is bad. You don't want to be just another applicant. Ergo, you don't want to write just another personal statement.

Make yourself stand out. We know you know this, but you will be competing against thousands of well-qualified applicants for admission to just about any law school. Consequently, your primary task in writing your application is to separate yourself from the crowd. Admissions committees will see innumerable applications from bright twenty-two year olds with good grades. Particularly if you are applying directly from college or if you have been out of school for a very short time, you must do your best to make sure that the admissions committee doesn't lump you in with everyone else who is your age and has basically identical credentials. Your essay presents an opportunity to put those credentials in context and to differentiate yourself.

Find your unique angle. The admissions people read tons of really boring essays about "how great I am" and "why I think there should be justice for everyone." Strive to find an angle that is interesting and unique to you. If what you write *isn't* interesting to you, we promise that it won't be remotely interesting to an admissions officer. In addition to being more effective, a unique and interesting essay will be far more enjoyable to write.

Who *are* you? Why are you different? What distinguishes you from others? Sometimes, applicants want to answer this question in a superficial way. They want to say, for example, "I am an Asian American from Missouri." That's probably a mistake. You should avoid the idea of fitting preconceived notions of identity. You almost never need to mention the honors and awards you've received. After all, there's a place for those on almost every law school application. It's called your resume, and repeating anything from it in your statement is nearly always bad juju.

Writer's Block?

Ask yourself this question: What experiences in your life have been the most meaningful and have most altered the course of your life? Try to express in a compelling manner some moment in your life, some experience you've had, or some intellectual slant on a personal interest. Try to relate this experience to your choice to attend law school.

Instead, you want to put yourself in a genuine context by explaining how your education, your personal and professional experiences, and the world around you have influenced you and your decision to attend to law school. Give the admissions officers a real frame of reference and real insight into the person you've become as a result of the experiences you've had. Be open about yourself. Don't just ramble on with clichés and platitudes. The more personal and individualized your personal statement is, the better received it will be.

In a nutshell (and in addition to the nuts and bolts like clarity, conciseness, and perfect grammar), admissions officers want to know *who you really are and what has made you the person you are today*. They look for introspection and the ability to reflect intellectually upon yourself and upon the experiences that led to the formulation of your attitudes and beliefs. Admissions officers look for individuals who understand their own strengths, weaknesses, and limitations. They look for people who have an awareness of their own pasts and who have learned from their own mistakes. They look for people who have grown intellectually and professionally and who want to grow some more.

Always **consider your audience.** A big part of your overall strategy should be to keep in mind what it would be like to be the reader. Ultimately, you are giving a portrait of yourself in words to someone who doesn't know you and who may never meet you, but who has the power to make a very important decision about the course of your life. Remember that it's a real person who will read your personal statement, though someone with real human traits who puts on his or her pants one leg at a time, just like you. Keep this person interested. Make this person curious. Make this person smile. Engage this person intellectually.

Loyola University Chicago

"The personal statement should describe an applicant's unique experiences and attributes that will enable the applicant to make special contributions to Loyola University Chicago School of Law, to the legal profession, and to society. The personal statement essay should be no more than two typed pages in length."

OUR POSITION ON WORK EXPERIENCE

Work experience in college. Most law school applications will ask you to list any part-time jobs you held while you were in college and how many hours per week you worked. If you had to (or chose to) work your way through your undergraduate years, this should come as good news. A great number of law schools make it clear that they take your work commitments as a college student into consideration when evaluating your UGPA.

Work experience in real life. All law school applications will ask you about your work experience beyond college. They will give you three or four lines on which to list such experience. Some schools will invite you to submit a resume. If you have a very good one, you should really milk this opportunity for all it's worth. Even if you don't have a marvelous resume, these few lines on the application and your resume are the only opportunities you'll have to discuss your post-college experience meaningfully—unless you choose to discuss professional experience in your personal statement as well.

Community service. An overwhelming majority of law schools single out community involvement as one of several influential factors in their admissions decisions. Law schools would like to admit applicants who show a longstanding commitment to something other than their own advancement.

It is certainly understandable that law schools would wish to determine the level of such commitment before admitting an applicant, particularly since so few law students go on to practice public interest law. Be forewarned, however, that nothing—*nothing*—is so obviously bogus as an insincere statement of a commitment to public interest issues. It just reeks. Admissions committees are well aware that very few people take the time out of their lives to become involved significantly in their communities. If you aren't one of them, trying to fake it can only hurt you.

If you have a legitimate history of community service and you choose to discuss community service in your personal statement, use it as a jumping-off point for discussing who you are. Also, it is incredibly important to discuss actual experiences you have had and how they affected your attitudes, your beliefs, and your life. Don't just discuss public service (or anything else) in the abstract.

Work experience and community service on your personal statement. The kind of job you've had or the kind of community service in which you have participated is not as important as you might think. What interests the admissions committee is what you've made of that job and what it has made of you. If you choose to mention a job you've had in your personal statement, you'll probably want to offer credible evidence of your competence and increases in responsibility. More important, use your work experience to give the admissions officer a frame of reference about who you are. How did that job change you and help you grow as a person? You also want to show off your professional experience within the context of your decision to attend law school.

What to Leave Out and What to Avoid

Don't repeat information from other parts of your application. The admissions staff already has your transcripts, your LSAT score, and your list of academic and extracurricular achievements. The personal statement is where you present all the *other* aspects of yourself in a meaningful way. Even if you don't mind wasting your own time, admissions officers will mind you wasting theirs.

In general, avoid generalities. Admissions officers have to read an unbelievable number of boring essays. Have we mentioned this already? You will find it harder to be boring if you write about particulars. It's the details that stick in a reader's mind. As Ludwig Mies van der Rohe once wrote, God is in the details.

Stick to the length that is requested. It's only common courtesy.

Even if no length is requested, don't get carried away. Although some law schools set no limit on the length of the personal statement, you shouldn't take their bait. You can be certain that your statement will be at least glanced at in its entirety, but admissions officers are human, and their massive workload at admissions time has an understandable impact on their attention spans. You should limit yourself to two or three typed, double-spaced pages. Does this make your job any easier? Not at all. In fact, practical constraints on the length of your essay demand a higher degree of efficiency and precision. Your essay needs to convey what kind of thinking, feeling human being you are, and page limitations allow for absolutely no fat.

Follow the directions. Somebody put a lot of thought into the language each individual law school uses to explain what it is looking for in a personal statement. Drafts were written and rewritten. Committees were formed. Resolutions were passed. Give them what they want.

Unless the directions say so, don't wax on about your goals. Face it: You have only an imprecise idea of what law school will be like. Everybody's goals change over the years. Your goals are especially likely to change because law school will change you. As you change and grow, your goals will morph. Leave the seventy-five-year plan out of your personal statement.

Maintain the proper tone. Your essay should be memorable without being outrageous and should be easy to read without being too formal or too sloppy. When in doubt, err on the formal side. Law school is kind of a stuffy place.

Don't try to be funny unless it's actually funny. An applicant who can make an admissions officer laugh never gets lost in the shuffle, and no one will be able to bear tossing your app into the "reject" pile. But beware! Most people think they're funny. (We think we're funny.) But only a few are able to pull off humor in this context.

Stay away from anything remotely off-color. Avoid profanity. It's not a good idea to be irreverent (although you will find at least one statement in this book that was a little naughty and got the person that wrote it into a top law school—or at least didn't keep him from gaining acceptance). Also, there are some things admissions officers don't need to know about you. Guess what these things are.

Circumvent political issues if possible. We can imagine a situation in which political issues might be unavoidable. If you worked for the Dole campaign in 1996 or the Gore campaign in 2000, or if you've been working at City Hall for a while now, then it makes some sense to discuss politics because it has been so central to your experience. You don't, however, want to write a polemic about your pet issue, no matter how near and dear it is to your heart.

Admissions officers don't care about your particular political viewpoints as long as they're thoughtful. They don't care if you are a Republican or a Democrat or about your position on the issue of gun control. But here's the problem: If you write about some political issue, you might look like the kind of person who is intolerant, unwilling to consider other viewpoints, and generally unpleasant. Who wants someone like that in their law school community for three years? And since lawyers must learn to think about issues from different angles, that kind of person is unlikely to make a very good lawyer. Be very careful.

Don't make religion the focal point unless you're applying to a law school with a religious affiliation. Don't misunderstand us. Religion is not taboo. It's fine to mention religion in any personal statement; just make it part of the whole. There is an obvious exception here. If you are applying to Baylor, Brigham Young, or Regent University, for example, then you may want to focus on religion because religion is very important at these schools.

Pepperdine University

"Pepperdine is a Christian university committed to the highest standards of academic excellence and Christian values, where students are strengthened for lives of purpose, service, and leadership. The School of Law seeks to further this mission, and encourages adherence to the highest moral and ethical standards.

How would you expect to contribute to this environment or identify with this mission?

Please include a brief personal statement indicating fully your reasons for wanting to study law, why you chose to apply to Pepperdine University School of Law, significant extracurricular and/or civic activities, and any further information which you feel should be considered by the Admissions Committee. If you desire, please discuss any applicable factors which would bring diversity to the class, including racial or ethnic origin, age, work experience, geographical origin, and socio-economic background."

Put the fraternity bake sale behind you. The same goes for the juggling club juggle-a-thon and the Womyn's Action Group all-night fundraising vigil. Achievements in a Greek organization or any club or student group are not the kind of life-changing events that have made you the person you really are today. If you were the editor of the school paper, or if you personally facilitated the temporary housing of more than 200 victims of domestic abuse over a three-year period—well, that's different. Tread cautiously. Make sure whatever you did rises to the level of having an actual impact on your life.

No gimmicks; no gambles. Avoid tricky stuff. You want to differentiate yourself but not because you are some kind of daredevil. Don't rhyme. Don't write a satire or a mocked-up front-page newspaper article. Gimmicky personal statements mostly just appear contrived and they fall flat, like a bad *Saturday Night Live* skit. As far as content goes, law schools don't like gimmicks. They don't like personal statements written as obituaries. Don't do the philosophical dialogue where you are a student of some Socrates who is asking you Really Profound Questions. Sure, you laugh. But we've seen it. Stick to a straightforward narrative.

SUBJECT MATTER TO AVOID IN YOUR PERSONAL STATEMENT

"My LSAT score isn't great, but I'm just not a good test taker." If you have a low LSAT score, avoid directly discussing it in your personal statement. Like the plague. Law school is a test-rich environment. In fact, grades in most law school courses are determined by a single exam at the semester's end (and occasionally even the year's end), and as a law student, you'll spend your Novembers and Aprils in a study carrel, studying your butt off, completely removed from society. Saying that you are not good at tests will do little to convince an admissions committee that you've got the ability to succeed in law school once accepted.

Consider also that a low LSAT score speaks for itself—all too eloquently. It doesn't need you to speak for it, too. The LSAT may be a flawed test, but don't go arguing the merits of the test to admissions officers because ordinarily it is the primary factor they use to make admissions decisions. We feel for you, but you'd be barking up the wrong tree there.

Save any mention of a low LSAT score for an addendum. (See page 28.)

"My college grades weren't that high, but . . . " This issue is a bit more complicated than the low LSAT score. Law school admissions committees will be more willing to listen to your interpretation of your college performance, but only within limits. Keep in mind that law schools require official transcripts for a reason. Members of the admissions committee will be aware of your academic credentials before ever getting to your essay. *Just like with low LSAT scores, your safest course of action is to save low grades for an addendum.*

Make no mistake: If your grades are unimpressive, you should offer the admissions committee something else by which to judge your abilities. Again, the best argument for looking past your college grades is evidence of achievement in another area, whether in your LSAT score, your extracurricular activities, overcoming economic hardship as an undergraduate, or your career accomplishments.

"I've always wanted to be a lawyer." Sure you have. Many applicants seem to feel the need to point out in their personal statements that they really, really want to become attorneys. You know better and you will do yourself a great service by avoiding such throwaway lines. Do not convince yourself in a moment of desperation that claiming to have known that the law was your calling since age six (when—let's be honest—you really wanted to be a firefighter) will somehow move your application to the top of the pile. The admissions committee is not interested in how much you want to practice law. They want to know *why*.

"I want to become a lawyer to fight injustice." Let's be clear: If you really want to spend your life battling for cosmic justice, by all means write your essay about it. Just keep in mind that there are a lot of people who will use this topic as well. Though some of these people really do want to fight injustice, way down in the cockles of their hearts, most just say that because they want to look good but are motivated to attend law school by less altruistic desires. Among the nearly 1 million practicing lawyers in the United States, there are relatively few who actually earn a living defending the indigent or protecting the civil rights of ordinary folks. Tremendously dedicated attorneys who work for peanuts and take charity cases are few and far between.

So here's the rub: Many essays about fighting injustice will appear obviously bogus and insincere. Even if you *are* sincere, you might get flung into the same pile as all the insincere phonies. Admissions officers will take your professed altruistic ambitions (and those of the hundreds of other personal statements identical to yours) with a chunk of salt.

If you can in good conscience say that you are committed to a career in the public interest, you must *show* the committee something tangible on your application and in your essay that will allow them to see your statements as more than hollow assertions. Speak from experience, not desire. This is where those details we've already discussed come in handy. If you cannot show that you are already a veteran in The Good Fight, don't claim to be. Also, do not be afraid of appearing morally moderate. If the truth is that you want the guarantee of the relatively good job that a law degree practically ensures, be forthright. Nothing is as impressive to the reader of a personal statement as the ring of truth. And what's the matter with a good job, anyhow?

ADDENDA

As previously mentioned, in addition to your personal statement, it may be a good idea to submit an addendum or two explaining certain unappealing facts about your application such as a low LSAT scores, low grades, or an arrest. In some cases, you may be required to submit an addendum explaining an incident in your past.

Q: How many times should you take the LSAT?

A: If possible, just once. It is better to have one score that shows true ability versus two scores.

Just the facts, and nothing but the facts. An addendum is *absolutely not* the place to go off on polemics about the fundamental unfairness of the LSAT or how that evil campus security officer was only out to get you when you got arrested. If possible, dryly point out that you have never done well on standardized tests but that it didn't stop you from maintaining a 3.8 grade point average in high school and a 3.6 in college. Whatever the case, lay out the facts, but let those reading draw their own conclusions. Be brief and balanced. Be fair. Be elegant. Be honest. Do not go into detailed descriptions of things. Explain the problem and state what you did about it. *Do not make excuses (even if they are completely legitimate excuses).* This is no time to whine.

Elegant

"adj. Characterized by or exhibiting refined, tasteful beauty of manner, form, or style."

—from *The American Heritage College Dictionary*

THE LOW LSAT ADDENDUM

If you have a low LSAT score, you might consider an addendum discussing it. You are never going to be able to completely mitigate a low LSAT score. The obvious and preferable alternative to an explicit discussion of a weak score would be to focus on what you *are* good at in your personal statement. If you really are bad at standardized tests, you must be better at something else, or you wouldn't have gotten as far as you have. If you think you are a marvelous researcher, say so. If you are a wonderful writer, show it. Let your personal statement implicitly draw attention away from your weak points by focusing on your strengths. There is no way to convince an admissions committee to overlook your LSAT score. You may, however, present compelling reasons to look beyond it.

Multiple LSAT scores, one good one. Let's say you took the LSAT twice. If you did much better in your second sitting than in your first, or vice versa, a brief explanation—if there is an explanation—couldn't hurt. If some adverse circumstance caused you to perform less than optimally, say so. Be honest. Be forthright.

Get to the point quickly. Bear in mind that your explanation may mean little to the committee, which may have its own hard-and-fast rules for interpreting multiple LSAT scores.

Acceptable Explanations for Low LSAT Scores

(1) Death in the family or other serious family emergency; (2) stressed over a work emergency; (3) serious illness. Note: Number 2 may backfire. Why didn't you reschedule?

Unacceptable Explanations for Low LSAT Scores

(1) Someone was hacking up phlegm next to you during the exam; (2) your first score was crappy, but then you took a class with The Princeton Review and it just skyrocketed; (3) you had a terrible hangover; (4) you had all this stuff going on but were too brainless to reschedule.

Good grades, bad LSAT score. If you have a history of poor standardized test scores but good credits, state as much candidly and cordially in a short, sweet, nondefensive addendum. All you really have to say is: "Standardized test scores don't predict my academic performance, and here is some evidence to back up my claim." It would be a nice touch if you could convince a college professor to write a letter on your behalf saying "this student has always had high grades but poor standardized test scores, so please disregard the scores."

THE LOW GRADES ADDENDUM

If you have lower college grades because you had to work at a real job in addition to going to college, because you had a child to feed, or for some other legitimate reason, don't be afraid to say so. It is much easier to argue a less than stellar record than a weak LSAT. In fact, it's imperative that you say so. Alternatively, let's say you started out as an aspiring electrical engineering major at Georgia Tech, promptly flunked out, then enrolled at Oglethorpe University, majored in English, and achieved a 4.0. Your cumulative UGPA is 2.85. You simply must write an addendum stating the facts of your situation fairly and honestly. There's a very good chance that you'll be pleasantly surprised at how easy it is to get admissions staffs to look beyond middling grades.

Telling the Truth

Don't lie on your law school application. If they ask you if you've been arrested, and you have been arrested, you must tell the truth. It's true that you'll probably have no trouble concealing those crazy things you did as an undergraduate from law school admissions staffs. There is, however, this thing called the bar exam at the end of the law school road. If the bar examiners find out you lied on your law school application, there is a high probability that you will never be allowed to practice law. After three years of law school and untold thousands of dollars invested in a legal education, wouldn't that just suck?

Q & A WITH ADMISSIONS OFFICERS

We interviewed admissions officers at five selective law schools about their applications in general and personal statements in particular. They revealed to us the specifics of how they and their staffs review applications; discussed essay themes, plagiarism, and deferrals, among other things; and offered writing tips to law school applicants. The following professionals generously offered their time to answer our questions:

Edward Tom, Director of Admissions for Boalt Hall School of Law, University of California—Berkeley

Dennis Shields, Associate Dean for Admissions and Financial Aid for Duke Law School

Andy Cornblatt, Dean of Admissions for Georgetown University Law Center

Robert Stanek, Associate Dean for Admissions and Financial Aid for The George Washington University Law School

Don Rebstock, Associate Dean of Enrollment, Management, and Career Strategy for Northwestern University School of Law

For ease of reading, we introduce each officer's response to the questions we ask with the name of the institution he serves.

WHAT THEMES CONTINUALLY APPEAR IN PERSONAL STATEMENTS?

Boalt Hall: The themes have changed over time because applicants are more aware of what we're looking for. The danger is that they all start to sound the same. Applicants need to be more strategic. Common themes are "Why I want to go to law school" or "I want to specialize in this area of the law." These and other themes haven't changed too much. We know a lot of people change their minds about what they want to do with their law degrees, so applicants need to think more globally. An alternate approach is to describe the journey you've been on since high school and to define the voice you have been developing along the way. This is a more generalized approach that can, if done well, summarize background, experiences, and academics.

Duke: What I see most often in essays is a recap of information found on the candidate's resume. This is not the most productive use of an admissions essay. I [also]

often see themes that start out, "I always wanted to be a lawyer because . . . ." What follows in the essay is seldom useful.

Georgetown: Part is usually autobiographical: "My commitment to service." This year, comments on September 11 and how that affected their careers and goals [were common]. Occasionally why they want to come to Georgetown and often all of these together, just a mixture.

George Washington: The majority [of personal statement themes center on] "Why I want to go to law school." "What I hope to do in the future" and also the autobiographical history [are popular themes].

Northwestern: The most common personal statements tend to be a chronology of their life, tragedies people have faced, and the standard "Why I want to go to law school."

WHAT WRITING TIPS WOULD YOU GIVE TO YOUR APPLICANT POOL?

Boalt Hall: First is to read the application directions. We look for quality of writing as well as substance. There should be no grammatical errors. If there are, I worry about how accurate they'll be in future practice. What if they misplace a comma in a multi-million-dollar contract? [But] write from the heart. Don't use a template or a book, as it becomes self-evident and artificial.

Duke: First I would say make sure the essay the candidate writes is school-specific. I see a number of essays that are generic as to the school for whom it is written.

Since law schools don't interview, the essay provides the opportunity for the candidates to present themselves in a meaningful way. You should not waste paper on information that is available in another part of your application. The trick is to find a context for the essay. The candidate needs to pick some experience that provides a frame of reference: a book, a job, a course they took, etc. Picking a particular experience or set of experiences makes it possible to write a short essay that is informative about the candidate. It's important that the essay be relevant to why they want to go to law school. It should be clear from the essay why law schools make sense for them.

Law schools want to bring a broad range of people in as students. So we are interested in how a given candidate is different in a significant way from many other candidates. Stay away from the check-the-box mentality. For example, "I'm an African American from Iowa." Saying only this and little more doesn't mean much. It is important to explain how such an experience has made you who you are and has influenced your interests and passions.

We have the transcripts and LSAT scores that speak to [the] candidate's intellectual aptitude for law school, but the essays can also shed some light on the intellectual ability of the candidate. How well can the candidate communicate her or his thoughts?

Georgetown: Be brief and focused. Part of the overall strategy is to write an essay keeping in mind what it would be like to be the reader. We're reading thousands of these; the notion of "the more, the better" defeats the purpose. Say what you have to say and be quiet. If you're reading a lot of these, you're grateful for the notion of brevity.

The more personal, the better, [and] the more individualized, the better. When you're done, ask a friend or family member [if they] know [you] better after reading it. I think if you were talking about yourself [or] your view [on some issue], real insight would be most successful in the personal statement.

George Washington: Proofreading is so obvious, yet forgotten continuously.

Northwestern: Stylistically make sure to check it closely. I've seen many [candidates] mess up with merges of law school names, i.e., "I want to go to 'X' law school because . . . ."

Focus on one or two main points. Go to the bookstore, to the management section about hiring people; there are questions in the backs of books [you'll find there] that you could answer.

My pet peeve is the generic personal statement. Applicants should tailor their statements to the school they are applying to. Show us that you did some homework on us.

We offer an open-ended question and two optional essays. The reason for the optional essay is because of the generic statements that we receive. The generic personal statement [is based on the] false assumption that schools are looking for the same thing.

WHAT DO YOU HATE TO SEE GRAMMATICALLY AND CONTENT-WISE?

Boalt Hall: Another law school's name mistakenly placed in the body of the personal statement sent to me. Carelessness is the kiss of death.

Duke: It ought to be well written. Let other people look at it before you submit it. It should be free of all grammatical errors. I don't like exceptionally long essays; get to the point in three or four pages unless there are unusual circumstances. If the candidate is older (thirty or forty years of age) or there are other unusual circumstances, then I'm willing to read more because they have experienced more. Avoid tricky stuff. I'd discourage applicants from using satire at the risk of it not being well received. I don't mind having religious beliefs in the essay, but it's not a good centerpiece. One guy wrote his personal statement in the form of an LSAT test question and responses. It was too gimmicky.

Georgetown: Grammatically: [I] hate to see people bungle the English language. Content: A paragraph form of the resume [and] the arrogance in expounding on the theories of the universe as if I'm anxious to know this.

George Washington: The worst offenses are misspellings, awkward construction, [and] incomplete sentences about which you would think candidates would take more care.

Northwestern: The generic one. The straight chronology. Uses of humor that don't work.

WHAT DO YOU LOVE TO SEE?

Boalt Hall: Don't only focus on the recent past. Explain how your experiences have helped your maturation process and what you have learned about yourself and about others. We're interested in more than just a list of experiences. I recommend they include a resume even if the application doesn't ask for it—as a way to chronologically sort their activities—so that time is not wasted listing all of this in the body of the personal statement.

Applicants should include an addendum to address specific topics or what they want to highlight. For example, an illness that caused their grades to slide, or a history of poor standardized test scores, in which case the applicant should include copies of their previous SAT or ACT scores.

Duke: I look for circumspection and introspection, a self-awareness, and a person who understands their strengths. The ability to engage intellectually, a sense of the role law plays in their lives. They don't have to know about law, but they should be thoughtful about it.

Georgetown: Openness. Someone who has given thought [to what he or she is writing]. To read something from an applicant who isn't afraid. For someone to give me a real sense of who they are, who isn't just rambling on.

George Washington: To learn history about the applicant, I prefer an autobiographical statement. I like to know what kind of person we're offering admission to.

Northwestern: I like to see demonstrated research about a school. I actually like personal statements that will have [a section] where they rattle off kind of neat components of their life, things that are unique that you don't see in applications but present life and tie into theme. [I also like to read about the] one significant thing in their life and how it has changed and influenced them.

WHAT BORES YOU?

George Washington: After twenty-eight years of doing this, there is a lot. From an applicant's standpoint, I'm less interested in their goals because I find it less helpful. I've seen a lot of goals change over the years. They don't know what law school is like [or have] only a vague idea of what it will be like.

Northwestern: The chronology.

WHAT TOPICS ARE RISQUÉ?

Boalt Hall: I think that humor, poetry, and unusual formats, such as court transcripts, should not be used. No jokes unless you're Jerry Seinfeld. Beautifully composed prose is best.

Duke: I don't care about their particular political viewpoints, as long as they're thoughtful about it. I'd like to see more ability to engage and accept other viewpoints while keeping your own view. I expect all students to be activists about something and share why they care about it.

Georgetown: I don't think there are any. I wouldn't call it risqué. In an effort to stand out, some try to be clever and gimmicky, and most [of these personal statements] feel contrived and flat. If you try and gamble with a poem, for every one that works ten are lame.

George Washington: It seems to be fashionable to discuss personal things, and I think applicants take "personal" too literally. There are some things I don't need to know and some things I'd rather not know about an applicant.

Northwestern: Humor and poetry are risky.

WHAT'S THE MOST RIDICULOUS ACHIEVEMENT YOU'VE EVER SEEN REFERENCED IN AN APPLICATION?

Duke: It's not like we pin people's resumes to their shirts. It all depends on the ability to say what's important to you. Depends on *how* they talk about it. How far have they come, having a sense of where they have been and what they've done?

This young woman—a white, middle-class woman—going to an Ivy League college asked me, "What can I say in an essay that would be helpful?" I asked her what kind of stuff she was involved in. She was on [the] swim team. "Why are you involved? Try to differentiate yourself. What motivates you to do a particular activity?"

George Washington: Achievements in a fraternity or sorority. I'm sure the effort was there, but somehow raising money through bake sales is not something they should list as a great achievement in life.

What steps do you take to recognize or prevent plagiarism (such as specialized software)?

Boalt Hall: We're aware of the [Web] sites. We do have a policy on plagiarism; anytime we see it we'll report to the misconduct committee.

Duke: Haven't yet. We're thinking about it. I don't think there's a great deal of plagiarism with law school [applicants].

Georgetown: It's a recognized threat, but we don't use software. But schools will have to start looking into this. We have the writing sample from the LSAT that we use.

George Washington: We haven't done a good job [of discovering] it. One reason is simply the volume we receive. Last year we had over 10,000 applications, and we just don't have time to double check. The only times when I became aware [of plagiarism] is if two personal statements are the same or know I've read it before. But there's no scientific way. Occasionally I'll come across something that doesn't ring true, that doesn't compare to their academic record.

If you had the option of doing away with personal statement requirements altogether, would you?

Boalt Hall: No. We're interested, particularly at Boalt, in human beings, not numbers. People have the opportunity to affect the lives of people. I find it irresponsible to look at a few numbers and make a decision.

Duke: No. I think in a perfect world we should interview everyone.

Georgetown: No. First, it gives me a sense of how well a person writes. And second, it gives us some things they've done that aren't in the application. That's helpful because we can't interview. This takes [the] place of that. Without this there's no freedom of expression, and for the seventy bucks they spend on the application fee, they deserve that.

George Washington: No. I find it to be a helpful part of the admissions process, sometimes more useful than the LSAT or the writing sample. The personal statement with the academic record gives me a good indicator of skills.

Do you prefer to receive online or paper applications and supplementary forms?

Boalt Hall: Paper. We don't take online applications. They can download the application [from our website], though.

Duke: We accept both. No difference, as long as it is in a timely fashion.

Georgetown: Online. We still get paper. Next year we'll be over half online and hopefully [that percentage will] continue to rise.

George Washington: No preference.

Northwestern: We now require online. We're the first law school to do this. The reason is that law school and the field of law require proficiency with computers, so we're preparing our applicants for this reality.

Do you or your staff read every personal statement that comes to you?

Boalt Hall: Yes. Every one.

Duke: They all get read.

Georgetown: Yes.

George Washington: Yes. How fully does it get read, though? Some grab you right away and you can make your decision right away, and with others, within a few paragraphs you can see what they're saying and you can make your decision immediately.

How many personal statements do you or your staff each read personally? What is the load? How much time do you dedicate to each application?

Boalt Hall: [For fall 2002 enrollment] we received about 6,900 applications and had six people reading more or less full time from the end of October through the end of March. On average, [we spend] at least ten minutes on each application.

Duke: Three full-time people read applications, along with two outside readers. Out of 4,100 applications, I read 3,000 of them and give fifteen to twenty minutes to each.

Georgetown: [We read] 11,500 total applications between myself and two others. How much time? It depends on the application. Some are easy. They're not all hard to do. The average length is forty-five minutes to one hour; some may take fifteen minutes, some three hours.

George Washington: We received 10,800 [for fall 2002 enrollment]. I do the first read on all and the final read on over three-quarters of all applications. This means I don't have free weekends from December to May.

Some are quick and some you agonize over. On average each application takes five to ten minutes.

Northwestern: We get 5,000. We each probably read about half of the overall pool.

WHAT SORT OF EXPERIENCE DO YOU REQUIRE OF THE PEOPLE WHO REVIEW APPLICATIONS? ARE THERE ANY PARTICULAR QUALITIES YOU LOOK FOR?

Boalt Hall: Our readers are associate and assistant directors at the school.

Duke: We hire bright people who will read carefully. We tell them to read more files; a lot of being a good file reader is context—being able to have the knowledge base. Full-time read 100 to 200 a week. Part-time read 50 to 100 a week. Outside readers look at 50 to 100 a week.

George Washington: A willingness to read. Some love to do it; others would rather pass it off to someone else. In general I keep the same committee from year to year. It speeds up the workflow. Every new member I have to train slows down the process.

HOW MANY APPS GO TO COMMITTEE?

Boalt Hall: Depends on the year.

Duke: Not many. Sometimes ten to twenty. The chair may see as many as 100.

Georgetown: We send 10 percent to the admissions committee and the rest are done within our office.

Northwestern: Most get two reads. Some get three. The first is done by the assistant director. If they vote waitlist, then [the] faculty gets [the] read, then me.

Is anything on the application really "optional"?

Boalt Hall: Only those items that are marked "optional."

Duke: No.

Georgetown: No.

George Washington: We don't require letters of recommendation, and that has to do with my own experience. I found it very burdensome after years of being out of undergraduate school to get these letters. It's rare to find a letter that changes the mind of the committee. Applicants' concern over letters is unwarranted.

Do applicants send extra material to you? If so, what is helpful? How much is too much?

Boalt Hall: We put aside CDs, videos, [and] senior theses.

Duke: Yes, loads of it, and it's put in an archived file. It's not useful. They think they should send their Ph.D. and honors theses. I'm not equipped to read all this. I've never watched a video or listened to a CD. Poetry is okay, but if it doesn't set you apart . . . I think it's rare that it works.

Georgetown: They can. If in doubt, send it. They send extra statements and letters. But don't send a thesis. The more you send, the more you dilute the product. Three letters is fine. Some have led complicated lives. Some forty year olds are working two jobs. In that case I don't mind a little extra.

George Washington: Yes, they do, and no, it's not always helpful. I receive copies of dissertations, compact discs, videos—all kinds of things. They're not as helpful as the standard package.

Northwestern: Sometimes. [The] reality is that there's no time [to review these materials]. Theses we don't read. We got a CD from an accomplished pianist that's actually in my briefcase.

THE LOW LSAT SCORE EXPLANATION: WHEN IS THIS NECESSARY? UNNECESSARY? HAVE YOU EVER GOTTEN ANY RIDICULOUS EXPLANATIONS THAT YOU'D LIKE TO SHARE?

Boalt Hall: If you have a low LSAT score and a history of poor standardized test scores, yet a very high college GPA, then you should talk about it. In an addendum, provide copies of previous standardized test scores. A lot of applicants claim they have a problem with standardized tests but don't provide proof. But an increasing number are providing copies of ACT and SAT scores to prove it.

Duke: The low LSAT . . . needs a poor test-taking history that disproves the predictive value of standardized tests for the candidate and the academic record that supports a contention. If there is a circumstance that was not optimal, write a paragraph. Say it quickly.

Georgetown: This is my recommendation for the low LSAT score explanation: Some have a history of poor standardized test scores, so in a nondefensive way send me a paragraph on standardized tests. Sometimes a letter from a professor or someone who can say, "This student has always had high grades but poor standardized test [scores], so please disregard the test scores." This sometimes works.

George Washington: The most valuable explanations are "I was sick" or "I had a family emergency" or "I was overwrought." Those explanations hold water if you have a second score that is improved. You can make [the] same explanation with the ACT or SAT score—that these aren't [predictive of] your performance. You do, however, have to have some evidence to back it up.

As far as ridiculous explanations: One wrote about a person chewing ice next to them; another had her period during the exam. Some come up with explanations that make me wonder why they're taking the test and not rescheduling. Too many feel that this is their last chance. They shouldn't. If you don't take it in October, take it in December or February. It is better to have one score that shows true ability versus two scores.

Northwestern: [A candidate should write an addendum about a] low LSAT only when there's been a history [of poor standardized test scores]. Provide a copy of [low] SAT scores so you can [show that your low LSAT score] obviously wasn't predictive. Divulge details of getting sick before or during the test.

DO YOU USE AN ACADEMIC OR SOME OTHER INDEX TO INITIALLY SEPARATE APPLICATIONS INTO "FOR SURE," "MAYBE," AND "LONG SHOT" PILES? DOES THE INDEX EVER PUT SOMEONE IN A "WHEN HELL FREEZES OVER" PILE?

Boalt Hall: We do use an index, but it's not used to separate applications. We read them in the order that they become complete.

Duke: We do have an index to help sort order. So, early in the year I want to read high ones and so on.

Georgetown: No. We read in the order they come in, so it's an advantage to apply earlier.

George Washington: We pull applications based on a completion date. All files completed are reviewed alphabetically. The index is based on GPA and LSAT score. The first thing I look at is the LSDAS report, and from there I can make an initial decision. So it becomes easier once I've formed this impression. If I feel a candidate is competitive, he better not blow it [with the personal statement] because I can be dissuaded. But in general [personal statements] do have an impact.

IF YOU HAVE AN APPLICANT WITH LOWER NUMBERS BUT A GREAT PERSONAL STATEMENT, WHAT DO YOU DO? IF A PERSONAL STATEMENT IS PARTICULARLY BAD BUT THE STUDENT'S GRADES ARE GREAT, WHAT THEN? IS THERE ANYTHING ABOUT A PERSONAL STATEMENT THAT MAKES YOU UNABLE TO TURN AN APPLICANT DOWN?

Boalt Hall: It puts them in a difficult situation because we're also looking for strong academic potential. You have to have strong numbers as well. I guess all law schools are looking for high academic potential in terms of academic talents, but we're also looking for interesting people, and that combination is what the admissions process is all about. The way the law is taught requires that there be different voices throughout our classrooms, but all of the people in that classroom must also have the academic ability to grasp the concepts, nuances, and issues that are being discussed. The caliber of the resulting dialogue is a function of that range of voices.

Duke: Someone who looks interesting in spite of not having a remarkable LSAT score or academic record—we would set [that] person aside and look later once we've read most of the files and have more candidates that are similarly situated to compare to them.

If bad [means] three sentences [for a personal statement] then they should be set aside.

The point is essays make a difference . . . when scores are similar. A good one will rescue a file we wouldn't typically seriously consider admitting.

Georgetown: It's hard to give a rule. This is what I tell students: If your goal is to jump the bar, GPA and LSAT set the bar. Everyone gets to jump, [and the] bar is never too high. No one in good conscience can tell you "Don't jump." Everyone has to jump. No matter how high the numbers are, you have to.

George Washington: Sometimes I'm convinced that this person is worth it regardless of record and some have been able to convince us. But usually it has to be about life experience and not just a well-written personal statement.

If you read something and find out [that this applicant is] a jerk, you don't want them around for the next three years. To a certain extent you're relying on objective factors after reading enough personal statements: whether they'd fit in, how well they'd be able to work with others.

**IF YOU DON'T AGREE WITH A STUDENT'S VOICE PHILOSOPHI-
CALLY, OR IF YOU KNOW THAT YOU DON'T WANT A CERTAIN
TYPE OF STUDENT ON CAMPUS—A TYPE THAT AN APPLI-
CANT CLEARLY SEEMS TO BE—HOW DOES THAT AFFECT
YOUR DECISION?**

Boalt Hall: We don't take political views into account at all in the admissions process.

Duke: The circumstance where I have a problem would have to do with some disciplinary problems that might make us pause. If their views are not in the mainstream, that might make them more interesting if it appears they would engage others in a positive way.

Georgetown: It makes no difference. They're not applying to be my friend or ideological soul mate. It's of no consequence.

George Washington: I don't have to agree politically [with an applicant] to offer [him or her] admission. I think there is a place for different views. If I feel that someone is a little beyond the pale I would not offer admission.

Northwestern: We don't let personal biases get in the way.

**HOW DO YOU FEEL ABOUT OTHER ACADEMIC CREDENTIALS?
DOES HAVING AN M.P.A., FOR EXAMPLE, BETTER A
CANDIDATE'S CHANCES OF ACCEPTANCE IF HE OR SHE HAS
A LOW UNDERGRADUATE GPA OR LSAT SCORE? DOES
COMING FROM A SPECIFIC, UNDERREPRESENTED-IN-LAW-
SCHOOL FIELD—LIKE ENGINEERING, FOR EXAMPLE—HELP
SOMEONE? HURT SOMEONE?**

Boalt Hall: A graduate degree is a big plus. I don't think [a candidate's major or profession] helps or hurts. It depends on the total package.

Duke: Bad academic records: It's a good idea to get a better record under your belt. Being older has a positive influence. In this era of high tech, I don't know that it helps, but . . . we do want representatives [from different fields]. Hard sciences: They're a little tougher. We're always thinking of the rigor of the [undergraduate] curriculum.

Georgetown: Anything [that] is an accomplishment is worthy. Is it good to have a grad degree? Yes. Trend in grades is important. That is, are grades on the rise [as the candidate progresses through school]?

George Washington: I'm very concerned with their academic records. I think that a person can overcome a problem. For example, if someone started and flunked out, then joined the military and became a 4.0 student afterward, so their combined average is 2.9—those are two different candidates. [If the candidate has] an outstanding career, I'm willing to look beyond the numbers. It is much easier to argue a less-than-stellar record than a weak LSAT [score]. The LSAT, for all of its faults, is the only record of how someone measures up to everyone else, and that is how it's applied, and it's hard to get around that.

One's major doesn't matter in the evaluation of an undergraduate record. When I read some of these majors, I can't understand what they're studying. I'm more willing to take lower grades in the classics versus the liberal arts [and] social sciences. But they're not underrepresented these days. Some we rarely see are drama and physical education. We wouldn't give extra points [to someone who majored in one of these subjects].

DO YOU HAVE A DESCENDING DEGREE OF IMPORTANCE OF APPLICATION REQUIREMENTS? THAT IS, IS THE LSAT THE MOST IMPORTANT MEASURE OF ABILITY? WHERE DOES THE PERSONAL STATEMENT FALL?

Boalt Hall: The personal statement is on par with the academic record and LSAT. If I were forced to assign weights, they would each be about one-third.

Duke: We don't. Every piece is equally important. We want every piece to be good.
Academics high; essay is an important component. They don't know what will jump out at the reader, so [they should] make sure it's all good. An applicant needs energy and time to fit the parameters of different schools; that's why I recommend applying to four to five schools, max.

Georgetown: There's no formula, but if forced to give an explanation, I'd break it into thirds: LSAT, [other] standardized tests, [and] undergraduate and graduate grades. And the subjective stuff: work experience and personal statement. It's not done mathematically, but they're each worth about a third.

George Washington: There are three parts of the application. I give equal weight to these three: personal statement, LSAT, and academic record. Letters hold no weight.

Northwestern:
1. LSAT
2. GPA
3. Interview
4. Work experience
5. Extracurricular leadership
6. Personal statements
7. Recommendations

THE APPLICANTS

We've broken down each of the following student profiles into several parts. First, you'll see the name of the student (unless they opted to publish their statement anonymously) and, if he or she provided one, a photograph. We then offer a short paragraph, composed primarily by the applicant, summarizing the major accomplishments and activities that he or she highlighted on his or her application. Next, we give you the student's stats, or statistical record (test scores, GPA), and demographic information (hometown, race, gender, class year). We list the law schools to which the student applied and the ultimate results of those applications. Finally, you will see the student's personal statement in its original condition—that is, with no corrections or excisions from the original document they submitted to the law schools. In a few cases, we printed more than one essay written by a student; Duke's application, for example, requires a Statement on Diversity in addition to the main personal statement.

We grouped applicants by the law school that they currently attend, recently graduated from, or will be matriculating into in the coming months. The law schools appear in alphabetical order. We have also included the statements of two people who were accepted to top law schools but have decided not to attend law school, at least not by the time we went to print. Their statements are in the Miscellaneous section of this part of the book.

While you read, you may want to consult each law school's profile, either in *Complete Book of Law Schools* or on our website, www.PrincetonReview.com. In each school's profile you will find information about students who applied to it in the most recent academic year, including the average LSAT scores, the number of applicants, and the yield (the percentage of students accepted who enrolled).

Anonymous

Anonymous was an English major at Columbia College of Columbia University with an average academic record over-all, though she made the Dean's List her last five semesters. She involved herself in speech and performance groups at Columbia. She worked in her native California for two years after graduation as a writer, editor, and designer, volunteer-ing for various nonprofit advocacy organizations. After decid-ing to attend law school, she left her job to travel.

Stats:
LSAT: 172
GPA: 3.5
College attended: Columbia University
Class: 1998
Hometown: Sebastopol, CA
Gender: Female
Race: White
Law school attending: Columbia Law School
Class: 2003

Applied to the following law schools:
Accepted: Cardozo School of Law, Duke, Fordham, NYU, University of California—Hastings, University of California—Los Angeles
Denied: Harvard, University of California—Berkeley (Boalt), Yale University
Other: None

Personal statement:
Anonymous said that there was no specific question that prompted her personal statement.

Often in my life, people have told me I'd make an excellent lawyer. It's been my impression that they rarely mean it as a compliment. Instead, they seem to mean that I'm overly argumentative, even bombastic, or that I insist on respecting even the smallest gradations of meaning as tantamount. I think I'd make a good lawyer (it should make for a rather poor essay if I didn't) too, for many of the same reasons. Argumentative, I read as curious about why people believe the things they do; bombastic, as a delight in the varied uses of the language; and insistence on slight distinctions in meaning, a desire for the best possible understanding. To these admirable qualities (if I do say so myself) I would add the pursuit of a rigorous intellectual detachment: the eternal desire and the frequent ability to see a situation not as my emotional loyalties or feelings would color it, but instead as it is. My attempts at detachment are often seen as cold, unfeeling, and even unfeminine, but it does not preclude emotion; it merely separates it from a rational understanding of any situation.

I don't mean to suggest I pursue a life where my emotion and my intellect are compartmentalized, nor that intellectual positions should be articulated without emotion. Much of what I believe is necessarily motivated by an emotional response to injustice or cruelty. But if I can't step back and investigate a case on its merits, lacking a wider perspective based firmly in rational discourse, I can't expect to successfully argue the point, nor can I expect others to understand. Often in the past when I'd made a too-hasty judgment, I became emotionally attached to it, and when asked to defend it, crumpled in tears as though I was being attacked, not my position. I'd feel horrible; I'd inadvertently put my opponent into a bind, for he or she had made me cry, and all common notions of decency precluded continuing the fight. I respected people more when they continued to argue, and didn't respond to my somewhat irrelevant display of emotion; if your beliefs are so attached to your emotions, perhaps you shouldn't be arguing about them in the first place. I remember my high school journalism teacher Mr. R— aghast at a similar display: our new principal, author of a multitude of unpopular reforms, was called upon by staff, students, and community members at a school board meeting to account for her actions; she looked out on her sea of detractors, placed her head in her hands, and began to cry. Mr. R— considered this the dirtiest move of all, but I wonder how much of her sobbing was premeditated, and how much was involuntary. These people were not attacking her, but asking her to defend her actions; that she couldn't separate the two, she should be faulted for, but to imagine her tears a pre-emptive strike against criticism she so richly deserved is to imagine her in a great deal more control of her emotions than I believe she was.

I think those who willfully use emotional blackmail are emotionally detached from their arguments, but perhaps not from the desire to win them. A construction so specific must have an particular person behind it, as indeed this one does: a college acquaintance of mine was always getting into fights where she was obviously and categorically wrong for the sheer joy of being contrary and willful, a practice to which I don't necessarily object. Instead, I objected to her characterization of everyone around her as overly argumentative and worse, out to get her or prove her wrong because we thought she was "dumb." She wanted to play, but didn't want to play fair, and could never admit she lost because her position was untenable. A laundry list of the positions she defended reveals arguments not driven by the firmest intellectual conviction but by the fieriest emotional desire to win. Every argument devolved into "you guys just think I'm stupid," and she lost everyone's respect; depending on sympathy for her victories, and blaming her losses on her opponents' supposed prejudices, she is also not the sort of arguer I aspire to be.

"Detachment is a rare virtue, and very few people find it lovable, either in themselves or others."

Gaudy Night, Dorothy L. Sayers

I started thinking about intellectual detachment as something to pursue through many readings and rereadings of *Gaudy Night* over the years, one of my favorite novels. In the book, the intertwined themes of intellectual detachment, devotion to one's work (usually academic or at the very least, intellectual) above all other considerations, and the importance of establishing truth at all costs play out in both the mystery story and the personal lives of the protagonists. Harriet Vane, who is told by Oxford don Miss De Vine that her detachment is a rare virtue, investigates a series of harassing letters and pranks at her (fictitious) old college, Shrewsbury. Concurrently, she agonizes over Lord Peter Wimsey's proposal of marriage, a choice that could mean the death of her vocation as a mystery-writer in favor of her vocation as a wife. Her confusion over the emotional turmoil in her life—turmoil of a particularly romantic nature—spills over into her present job of clearing up the mystery, and she is unable to recognize the criminal's antagonism towards professional women. Instead, she "eagerly peopl[es] the cloister with bogies": imagining that celibacy drives one into the particular sort of madness behind the "Poison Pen" letters. The implication seems to be that because she mucks it up so dreadfully, while Lord Peter sails in and saves the day by solving the mystery, that it isn't her proper job in the first place: unable to detach her emotions from her work, she can't see the forest for the trees. When it comes to writing her novels and her academic papers, however, she is able to do her job well, even at great cost to her emotional calm.

I don't wish to end by suggesting that I or indeed anyone else should wreak great emotional pain in the pursuit of academic or intellectual purity or strength, but instead that in order to do my job well, especially the job of lawyering, I must try to understand my conclusions in rational terms, no matter how much emotion drives me, and perhaps should drive me, to my conclusions.

Jason Amster

Jason Amster was a copy chief with Network Computing and was a journalist for almost ten years before attending law school.

Stats:

LSAT: 171

GPA: 3.4

College attended: SUNY—Stony Brook; Master of Science in journalism from Syracuse University

Class: 1992; master's degree, 1993

Hometown: Long Island, NY

Gender: Male

Race: White

Law school attending: Columbia Law School

Class: 2005

Applied to the following law schools:

Accepted: Columbia, Fordham

Denied: None

Other: NYU (placed on waitlist, withdrew application)

Personal statement:

(For Columbia)

"Candidates to Columbia Law School are required to submit a personal essay or statement supplementing required application material.

"Such a statement may provide the Admissions Committee with information regarding such matters as: personal, family, or educational background; experiences and talents of special interest; one's reasons for applying to law school as they may relate to personal goals and professional expectations; or any other factors that you think should inform the Committee's evaluation of your candidacy for admission."

"This statement should be printed on a supplementary sheet or two and should be returned to the Law School with other application materials."

About three years ago, a frightful brush with a libel suit rekindled my long-dormant desire to be a lawyer. As Sunday editor of a midsize daily newspaper, I copyedited a story and wrote an accompanying headline about a survivalist camp that was in a tax dispute with the town. The camp was training its members in the use of firearms, survival skills and military tactics on a local tract of land. Soon after the story ran, my managing editor called me into his office and told me this group was suing the newspaper over the story and had specifically cited the headline, which characterized the camp as "militant." He and the executive editor assured me the coverage and headline were fair. Even so, I began to fear for my job. Sensing my concern, the managing editor had me meet with the newspaper's lawyer, who shared my boss's confidence. The lawyer was reassuring and, as I realized later, inspiring, as he discussed libel laws and his daily role in defending the newspaper and other clients.

This experience taught me more than the importance of careful word choice. It reminded me how close I had come to following other career paths and of the lessons that would eventually guide me to law school.

About 10 years earlier, I chose to major in engineering as a college freshman. I did this not because I felt a calling but because engineering seemed like an impressive vocation. And that's what I believed was the point of a career: to impress people. Although I survived the rigors of first-year college engineering classes, impressing people turned out to be insufficient motivation to truly excel. But then came a turning point: an upper-level class in Shakespeare. Verbal analysis, writing, discussion? At last something felt natural. I abandoned engineering and followed my heart through academia: social sciences, literature, religion, studying abroad. I learned the fulfillment that comes in pursuing my interests.

Toward the end of my undergraduate studies, I found myself torn between careers in law and journalism. Both fields' emphasis on communication, public service and the truth were appealing. Although law exerted the stronger emotional pull, I chose journalism because I felt better prepared for it. But in fact, I wasn't entirely ready for journalism either. I had yet to learn the true value of hard work and focus.

In my first jobs after graduate school, I was distracted by the thought that advancement should be easier. Was I out of my league? Did I belong in this career? My concerns mounted until I tried a new tact: I would focus not on reward, but on the task at hand. Every sentence I wrote or edited would be as perfect as I could make it. With that new strategy, I achieved the success that had been eluding me: At Dow

Jones Newswire, I was promoted from copy reader (junior reporter) to editor in only a year, a unique achievement. My self-confidence grew as I advanced to new responsibilities in new positions.

Indeed, the lawsuit was a rare dark moment in an otherwise joyful career. Fortunately, my anxiety over the suit was brief. The newspaper quickly prevailed, and I remained a valued editor, though I now saw myself as powerless. I was forced to watch from the sidelines while the lawyers waged the real battles. My passion for the law grew, but I hesitated from taking the leap. A final epiphany gave me the push I needed.

About a year after the libel suit, my son was born. It was a time of happiness and introspection. I wanted my son to benefit from the lessons I've learned, but what wisdom could I possibly impart? It now seemed simple: If you pursue your interests and work hard at them, confidence and success will follow. Don't be afraid to follow your heart.

If I can give this advice, I must take it as well.

Michael Brueck

In addition to serving as a presiding officer and board member on his university's student honor council, Michael held the positions of treasurer and newsletter editor of the College Republicans and was a member of several campus honor societies, including the pre-law society on campus. A finance and international business double major, he completed internships at a financial services firm and a retail bank as an undergraduate. Upon graduation, he worked for one year as a client accountant with the law firm of Skadden, Arps, Slate, Meagher & Flom.

Stats:

LSAT: 172

GPA: 3.61

College attended: University of Maryland—College Park (Finance and International Business)

Class: 2001

Hometown: Harrington Park, NJ

Gender: Male

Race: White

Law school attending: Columbia Law School

Class: 2005

Applied to the following law schools:

Accepted: Columbia, Fordham, Georgetown, NYU, University of Chicago

Denied: Harvard, Stanford

Other: Cornell (withdrew application), University of Pennsylvania (placed on waitlist)

Personal statement:

(For Columbia)

"Candidates to Columbia Law School are required to submit a personal essay or statement supplementing required application materials.

"Such a statement may provide the Admissions Committee with information regarding such matters as: personal, family, or educational background; experiences and talents of special interest; one's reasons for applying to law school as they may relate to personal goals and professional expectations; or any other factors that you think should inform the Committee's evaluation of your candidacy for admission.

"This statement should be printed on a supplementary sheet or two and should be returned to the Law School with other application materials."

"You're ruining my life," the respondent whimpered, tears streaming down the cheeks of his distraught face as they had been for the last two hours. From across the room, his family looked on. "I have done nothing wrong, and now you're taking everything away from me."

I was used to dealing with emotionally fragile respondents during Student Honor Council hearings, but this person stood out. He was perhaps the most dejected and physically shaken I had encountered, requiring frequent adjournments to regain his composure. I felt empathy for him, as I had for all respondents during hearings. They all reacted in different ways: some with anger, some with fear, others expressing hopelessness. It was my job to ensure that, regardless of any emotional overtones, all sides of a case were fully heard. Doing my job right required disregarding my emotions, but that was often easier said than done.

At the University of Maryland, when an infraction of the Code of Academic Integrity is alleged, an honor hearing is convened to adjudicate the matter. The Presiding Officer leads and directs these hearings, which can involve as many as 20 participants, including professors, students, attorneys, and family members. The Presiding Officer is depended upon to provide procedural authority and must have intimate knowledge of all relevant rules and their proper applications. In addition, he or she must initiate the questioning of respondents, lead deliberations with other board members, and draft written opinions after each hearing that must withstand the scrutiny of the appeals process and, in some cases, legal action.

When I first joined the Honor Council as a Board Member, my main intention was to build skills for a career in the law, and my experience has greatly improved my abilities in dispute resolution, mediation, leadership, and communication. I also joined for some of the same reasons for which I wish to pursue a life in the law: intellectual challenge in a demanding and meaningful atmosphere, and the opportunity to continuously grow as a critically thinking person. However, the more involved I became with the organization, the more my personal goals yielded to our mission of promoting academic integrity on campus. Inevitably, during the course of that mission, punishments were dealt. Peoples' lives were altered; their academic careers were sometimes ended. In the view of some respondents, we were ruining their lives.

Those of us on the Honor Council knew we were not perpetrators of an offense upon the respondents; we were only administering the rules. I never doubted that the cases our Board had worked on had been handled accurately and professionally. We made great efforts and spent many hours deliberating to explore every angle, assuage every doubt, and ensure that the evidence was fully supportive of our decisions. However, two years of deep involvement in such a group had begun to take an emotional toll.

Since starting my tenure on the Honor Council, I had felt misgivings about being in a position in which I was asked to judge my peers. My reservations had been manageable, but after that night's hearing, they had reached an unbearable crescendo. I felt my sense of duty clashing directly with my sense of compassion and felt torn between two essential principles. I no longer wanted to be in a position that controlled the fate of another, regardless of what the rules were. I kept envisioning that respondent's sobbing, pleading face, and even though I hadn't placed him in his position, I couldn't help but feel a sense of responsibility for his situation.

There was no definitive event that ushered me back into full acceptance of my duty. It was a gradual process of internal conflict, shaping and reshaping my ideology case by case until I once again knew in my heart what I had always known in my head: that the administration of justice is not a burden but an honor, and that doing what is right does not always mean doing what is easy. Throughout this process, I reaffirmed that the enforcement of our academic standards and compassion for others are not mutually exclusive concepts. My determination was strengthened by elevating my standards of personal responsibility and respect for my community far beyond that which was required of me by rule, for only by exceeding those requirements could I feel more comfortable enforcing them. The knowledge that I was making a positive impact on campus overshadowed my previous sense of doubt. My outlook gave me the mental strength to make difficult decisions with confidence and to feel at peace with myself in doing so.

The law is a profession that demands the ability to make critical decisions that impact the lives of others. Throughout a career in the law, the lessons I have learned will surely be put to the test, and I am ready for that challenge. When asked what the most important thing I learned in college is, I proudly respond, "honor."

Emma Grewal

Emma held several leadership positions for various international and student groups while in college. Emma graduated from the University of Florida with a degree in political science and economics. She interned with the State Department before starting law school in the fall of 2002.

Stats:
LSAT: 163
GPA: 3.85
College attended: University of Florida—Gainesville
Class: 2002
Hometown: Plantation, FL
Gender: Female
Race: Asian
Law school attending: Cornell Law School
Class: 2005

Applied to the following law schools:
Accepted: Cornell
Denied: None
Other: None

Personal statement:
Emma did not write her personal statement in response to a specific prompt.

At the age of 66 days I was offered the first of many extraordinary opportunities – to travel and live abroad. When I went to India with my mother, I lived a culture and lifestyle different to the one that I am accustomed to now. This was the beginning of my love for international people, travel, and affairs. Over the years, I have traveled to many countries including Kenya, Argentina, the Dominican Republic, and France. Each country that I have visited has encouraged me to be a true global citizen – one that has a deep understanding of international people, cultures, practices, and laws. As the world becomes more intertwined and interdependent, my skills with diversity and my multicultural educational background will aid in a pursuit of a career in international law.

My interest in international affairs extends to the University of Florida activities with which I am currently involved. Volunteers for International Student Affairs (VISA) is the largest, most diverse student organization at the University of Florida with a mission to promote cultural awareness to the student body. As Vice President for International Affairs, I serve as a liaison to the International Center, Hispanic Student Association, Black Student Union, and Asian Student Union.

The most interesting aspect of working with VISA is not learning more about my culture, but rather learning about other traditions and viewpoints. For instance, through VISA I have learned that in Palestine, there is a significant population of Christians whose life experiences are significantly different from Palestinians of other religions. VISA allows me to gain experience working with international students and organizations to understand and resolve the unique situations arising from an international environment.

Coming from a family that is originally from India, I have a different set of life experiences than other people. My culture is an important part of who I am and helps me better relate to people of other cultures and backgrounds. Through my experience living in India, and my numerous trips since, I understand the issues and problems that exist in developing countries and that people of these countries face.

Even though I have a great interest in international affairs, I love being an American. Sometimes I feel as if I am not considered an American because of my skin color or heritage, but my heritage makes me appreciate America even more. I have lived in another country so I know how original and special America is. Although America is a blending of different cultures and ideas, which could be a cause for massive social unrest, America overcomes these differences to create a united society found nowhere else in the world.

Especially in light of the World Trade Center tragedies, I feel even more proud to be an American. I helped VISA sponsor a series of discussions with 'Islam on Campus' to promote unity among people of all faiths, as well as a fund-raiser for Afganistani refugees.

One of the reasons I would like to study international law is so that I can show my love for America. I want others to know of my deep pride for America and the principles that it stands for by working for an international organization. I hope to one day help write international laws and treaties that incorporate American ideals of fairness and justice. As the world's people become more mutually dependent and nations' borders are diminishing, the world will require a more cohesive system of law to ease the transition of globalization.

I will bring maturity, intelligence, and a determined interest in international affairs when I pursue my legal education. My diversity and extensive experience in multicultural issues will be an asset that will be a unique contribution to Cornell University School of Law.

Caroline H. Ryan

As the chair of the Williams College Student Activities Council, Carrie doubled its operating budget, tripled its events calendar, and spearheaded a project to renovate and run a student lodge/pub. She was also an elected officer on the College Council, was admitted into the Gargoyle Honor Society, was an alternate Fulbright Scholar, completed an honors thesis on the personal essay—the first of its kind— made the Dean's List, and was a member of various sports teams. After graduating from college she worked first as the assistant technology director, and then as a paralegal, in a local law firm. She is a member of the Romance Writers of America, has completed two novels, and has designed and run a large romance-writer Web community.

Stats:

LSAT: 168
GPA: 3.4
College attended: Williams College
Class: 2000
Hometown: Greenville, SC
Gender: Female
Race: White
Law school attending: Duke Law School
Class: 2005

Applied to the following law schools:

Accepted: Duke, Emory, University of Richmond, University of South Carolina, University of Virginia, Wake Forest University, William and Mary
Denied: None
Other: None

Personal statement:

(From Duke Law School's application)

"Every applicant is required to submit a personal statement of no more than

two pages. The statement is your opportunity to introduce yourself to the admissions decision maker and should include:

- what you think have been your significant personal experiences thus far beyond what may be reflected in your academic transcripts and on your résumé, and
- your personal and career ambitions.

From your personal statement, we should be able to understand why you want to go to law school and why you have decided to apply to Duke."

Torts vs. Tarts

It was three o'clock on a Saturday morning, and I had just finished typing a paragraph when it hit me: this was the end. I tinkered with the spacing of the lines, calculating the page count (and subsequent word count) from various angles, each time falling within the editorial guidelines for a single-title romance novel of 90,000 – 110,000 words.

I shrugged, yawned. Waited for the choir of angels to sing, but nothing. And so I just went to bed. Even today, a year and another novel later, I'm not sure I truly appreciate the achievement of finishing my first manuscript. However, I do understand the accomplishment of dedicating myself and working hard to achieve a lofty goal. Furthermore, I recognize how this accomplishment can translate into other areas of my life, including law school.

Not many people would draw a comparison between writing a romance novel and practicing law, but there are similarities, not the least of which is a collection of misconceptions held by those outside the profession. Just as most non-romance readers claim that all romance novels are the same - trashy and formulaic - many laymen proclaim lawyers as an ambulance-chasing hoard.

It doesn't help that to the uninitiated writing a romance novel seems to be a simple task: take a guy and a girl, put them somewhere in time, give them a conflict, make them fall in love, rip them apart, reconcile them in the last four pages. But as a fellow writer once said, "Saying all romance plots are boilerplate is like saying there is only one land route from DC to San Francisco." Crafting a believable story is as difficult as crafting a case – there must be a logical flow to the events, there must be motivation and consequence, and when all is said and done every loose end must be satisfactorily tied.

Add to this mixture an extremely knowledgeable and dedicated demographic of readers, and, as in law, writing a novel begins to entail a tremendous amount of research. Romance readers know their history, and are for the most part unforgiving of those writers who do not know theirs. Hence, research becomes vital if one does not want to horrifically embarrass oneself.

Perhaps the most obvious similarity between writing a romance novel and practicing law is the actual writing itself. While the words employed in a romance novel are vastly different from those used by lawyers (excluding divorce settlements, of course) if the stacks of files on my desk at work are any measure, the amount of writing in both endeavors is commensurate. Indeed, the first lesson I ever learned as both a writer and a paralegal is that paper fuels each profession.

Finally there is the passion. Not the kind of passion that most people associate with romance novels, but the passion of pursuit. Law School is demanding, and hard work and dedication is necessary. But true dedication, the kind that can keep you awake working until 3:00am Saturday morning, must have a root in passion - a desire to learn and push forward. I feel that this will be my greatest contribution to Duke Law School: a passion for knowledge that extends beyond the classroom walls to my family, to my community, and to life itself.

Back to that early morning when I finally typed "The End." Was I proud? Undoubtedly so. Did I fully understand my accomplishment? Unfortunately no. It was never an option for me to NOT finish my first novel. Furthermore, the end was just another beginning. There were publishers and agents to query, not to mention over 400 pages of editing and re-editing and re-re-editing. In that regard, finishing my first manuscript seemed to be just one step in the course of many. But I do know that in the process of achieving this goal I have learned lessons that will serve me well through law school and beyond: how to dedicate myself and work hard; how to write and persevere. And finally, how to enjoy the process.

Statement of diversity:

(For Duke)

"Diversity Essay (not to exceed two pages).

"Because we believe diversity enriches the educational experience of all our students, Duke Law School seeks to admit students from different academic, cultural, social, ethnic and economic backgrounds. If you choose to submit this essay, tell us how you think you would contribute to the intellectual and social life of the law school."

Average

I should be considered average – I'm sure most people think of me as such. I'm a white woman from an upper middle class family, the youngest of three daughters with divorced parents. I attended a private Episcopalian high school where I was top of the class, but was still considered average.

From Williams I graduated with high marks. I occasionally took five classes – one more than was considered normal. I had the normal disappointing first semester during my freshman year that I then overcame in the spring. I ran a few college clubs and was active in campus politics, but every student made their mark in some way or another. After graduation I did what many college graduates do: worked for a boarding school for a year before choosing a profession. Average.

And yet, as much as I should be average I've never felt average. I have helped autopsy bodies from murder scenes that I helped investigate. I've walked on ancient Mayan palace floors that I uncovered with my hands. I've written two novels and walked five miles out of the Wind River Mountains with a split knee and a hip-to-toe leg brace made from a sleeping pad and two large sticks. But then again, everyone has his or her accomplishments – at least everyone in my world does.

Perhaps that is why I am able to feel extraordinary and yet be considered average – because I live in a world where accomplishment is the norm. I grew up in a family in which attending college was never a question and pursuing a career in law is whole-heartedly supported. In my world, achieving lofty goals is the expectation.

Technically I could be considered a minority – my grandparents being born in and my mother being raised on a banana plantation in South America. Technically I could call myself Latina. But I don't, because that is not how I choose to define my diversity. In my mind diversity can't be claimed of grandparents who I never knew nor of a lifestyle in which I was never raised.

Instead I claim diversity in the variety of my experiences; that I am a painter, a Vietnam War buff, and a Southern Debutante at the same time. That I know how to sail, how to knit, and how to shoot a rifle. That I am not only open to new ideas and experiences, but also one who seeks them out.

Greg Kanyicska

Besides making the Dean's List every semester and holding down a job with the State of Florida throughout his four years of undergraduate study (as well as one year post-undergrad and one year prior), Greg also managed to keep the nascent hopes of a literary career alive. As if that weren't enough—and it isn't—Greg also manages to make his friends laugh more often than not.

Stats:
LSAT: 176
GPA: 3.81 (communications)
College attended: Florida State University
Class: 2002
Hometown: Tallahassee, FL
Gender: Male
Race: White
Law school attending: Duke Law School
Class: 2005

Applied to the following law schools:
Accepted: Duke
Denied: Cornell, Harvard, Stanford, University of California—
Berkeley (Boalt), Yale
Other: None

Personal statement:
According to Greg, he didn't think the prompts for his essays "went beyond the usual 'tell us about yourself' and 'include a statement of diversity' thing."

I promise I won't keep you long. You probably have a pounding headache reading through all these statements, and I wouldn't want to keep you from a real gem buried in the pile.

I nearly had this done about a month ago. I had it composed in my mind, but I never wrote it down. No doubt it would've been out of date by now, as everyday I seem to reach some new revelation about myself. I've done a lot of self-reflection over many years and I like to think that I see myself more clearly than most people see themselves.

Actually, while that would seem to make sense, it seems the more I learn the less I know and it is those who haven't a clue as to who they are see themselves most clearly, though perhaps not accurately. The quest for understanding is an infinite string of questions and the answer to "Who is Greg Kanyicska?" is an essay without end. . . or beginning it appears, but since I promised to be succinct I'll get on to it.

Like most people, or at least everyone I know, I was born. My entrance came in the middle of February 1979 at a state-run hospital in Miskolc, Hungary. Though pretty much everything was state-run in socialist Hungary I managed to stay out of politics throughout my formative years. Then, in 1986 my family moved to Tallahassee, Florida for a year. That year has stretched to nearly sixteen.

I've managed to survive life in the South through my charm and wit, and an immeasurable capacity for learning (and hyperbole). In that time I've also managed to grow up, somewhat, and to grow restless. My desire to leave and find myself (isn't that what people do?) has finally exceeded the level of comfort and familiarity I've found here.

Well, that's enough bio, I'm still young and hope to have most of my life still ahead of me, and I'll skip the academic stuff; it's too boring. If you're interested it should all be in my app.

Now for the big finish, I'll start with an open-ended statement, and then promptly close it. Greg Kanyicska is: bad with names, but good with numbers; good company, but bad with introductions; good with language, but bad at writing things down; a one time poet, now without a muse; always a dreamer, though often disenchanted; and finally, done, so that you can go on to find that gem that's waiting somewhere down the pile. (If you enjoyed this however, I've included some further reading for your pleasure.)

Statement of diversity:

If you're looking for a "straight, white male" read no further, I qualify. If, however, you have some reservations, then please allow me to elaborate.

By "straight" I mean I am heterosexual, but I'm a non-practicing heterosexual, or perhaps I practice too much and don't participate enough. But enough about the frustrations in my life, lets go on to "white." (I personally don't believe in any such labels, except, in that as others believe in them and lend credence to them, they gain a significant power. Human beings cannot help but categorize; without our fabricated reference points we'd go insane).

Getting back to being "white," I was born in Hungary and spent the first seven years of my life there. I'm pretty sure that my ancestry is mostly Caucasian for a good ways back through history, but my saving grace is that I am a foreigner and not locally grown.

As for being "male", there isn't much there to work with. I'm ~5'11", 160 lbs., brown hair, grey eyes, not unattractive, my hobbies include sailing, writing, sketching and getting carried away by my sense of humor [hopefully I caught you in a good mood].

Religion: none. I'm not Atheist, because Atheism has become a religion as dogmatic as all the rest. I am meditative and contemplative and have come to my understanding of god, the universe, and myself by starting out abandoning as many prejudices and preconceived notions as I could.

I am a semi-literate intellectual, and have grown to accept that even contradictory statements may be true. It is, therefore, not out of the realm of possibility that even an average "straight, white male," like myself, cannot help but add to the diversity of any setting.

Michael Dallal

After receiving a Bachelor of Science with honors in mechanical engineering from Hofstra University, Michael ob-
tained a Master of Engineering in mechanical engineering
from The Cooper Union for the Advancement of Science and
Art in 2001. His GPA earned him the Republic Aviation Assistance Award and led to his repeated naming to the Dean's List.
During the past three years and concurrent with his graduate
studies, Michael has worked full-time as an acoustical and
structural dynamics engineer and as an acoustical consultant
to the New York City Department of Design and Construction.
He has also remained active in his hometown of Great Neck,
New York, helping to found a synagogue that brings together
those who share his Iraqi-Jewish heritage.

Stats:

LSAT: 163
GPA: 3.40
College attended: Hofstra University; Master of Engineering
    from The Cooper Union
Class: 1999; master's degree, 2001
Hometown: Great Neck, NY
Gender: Male
Race: Jewish, Iraqi American
Law school attending: Fordham Law School
Class: 2005

Applied to the following law schools:

Accepted: Brooklyn Law School, Fordham

Denied: Columbia, NYU

Other: Benjamin N. Cardozo School of Law (placed on waitlist)

Personal statement:

Michael advises that there was no specific prompt for which his statement was written, only that it was "restricted to two (2) single-spaced pages."

While researching and writing my Master's thesis, I discovered how I could best utilize my knowledge and experience in engineering for the benefit of society. My thesis focuses on the effects, regulation and mitigation of construction noise. It is based upon a research project that I performed with the New York City Department of Design and Construction, and it was published and presented at national meetings of the Acoustical Society of America. By comparing noise regulations from around the world and measuring sound levels at construction sites in the New York area, I found that many current noise regulations in the United States are inadequate, vague and impractical. Residents neglect to ensure their own auditory safety while construction projects are in progress, and they focus only on filing complaints against the projects. Unfortunately, these complaints are rarely followed. In addition, construction managers and contractors consistently neglect community environmental and noise regulations, and environmental regulations are only specified in construction contracts covering long duration projects. I also found that environmental regulations and their enforcement fall far short in the United States in comparison to those of Asia and the European Union. As part of my research, I was charged with proposing specific, enforceable specifications and guidelines for construction bids that are currently in the process of being adopted for New York City street construction projects. Due to time and budget constraints, detailed environmental specifications cannot be written for all projects. Nevertheless, citizens must be protected from environmental damage at all times and not only during ongoing construction. Modern society needs to further its development of environmental law and community regulations in order to expand its increasingly demanding goals for protecting citizens from environmental hazards. It is imperative that regulations are practical, easily monitored and continually updated to consider new technologies that reduce the cost and increase the performance of environmentally friendly products. An attorney who knows both environmental law and developing technology is best qualified for this undertaking.

My academic journey to this point has been rather circuitous, spanning such diverse disciplines as medicine, theology, and acoustics, each of which has helped formulate my interest to use law and engineering to improve the environment. I spent my formative years in Tehran, Iran before moving to the United States. In my new country, I was struggling to master the English language while speaking both Farsi and Arabic at home, while other children were excelling in any number of academic areas. As I began to excel in school and to show a talent for mathematics and science, I was encouraged by everyone in my family to become a doctor. Therefore, I began my undergraduate education studying the sciences at Columbia University. Moreover, because my parents had always emphasized the importance of exploring our historical and cultural background, I simultaneously studied Jewish law and Hebrew text at the Jewish Theological Seminary. Although I enjoyed my introductory science courses and was successful in Judaic studies, it became clear to me that I was following an academic path that had been selected for me, and not one that I had selected. My growing discontent was exacerbated in the fall of 1994 by the death of my cousin, who was nothing less than a brother to me, in a senseless automobile accident. My spirit and my desire to learn were nearly destroyed. I transferred to Hofstra University in order to be as close as possible to my grieving family, as my focus was completely on loss, and academics were no longer important.

After a grueling year, I motivated myself to direct my energies back to my academic endeavors. In the spring of 1996, I selected engineering as a vocation and also became an active leader in the Hofstra community. I was tapped for Theta Tau Professional Engineering Fraternity and later became President of my chapter and National Outstanding Student Member. I organized outreach events including two engineering competitions for 70 high school students throughout Long Island. To help my peers, I coordinated a regional conference at Hofstra for 50 university students from the Atlantic seaboard and tutored others in a wide range of courses. My academic efforts were recognized by the Hofstra administration and generated my induction into the Kappa Mu Epsilon National Mathematics Honor Society. Concurrently, I remained and continue to remain involved with my Jewish heritage. My family and I helped to found our community's synagogue, where I later met and married my wife, Loretta.

Since receiving my bachelor's degree with honors, I have been working full time in the engineering field and will earn a Master of Engineering degree from The Cooper Union for the Advancement of Science and Art in December 2001. I also passed the National Council of Engineers for Engineering and Surveying examination to become a New York State certified intern engineer. My employment thus far has allowed me to analyze various structures from bridges to naval ships and submarines, as well as to utilize my knowledge of acoustics to design music studios and concert halls. I was most fortunate to have been given the opportunity to assess the safety and potential structural damage of buildings that may have been impacted by the destruction of the World Trade Center on September 11, 2001. I am currently strengthening my experience with international environmental regulations while working with Physicians for Social Responsibility by investigating the development of alternative energy production and consumption requirements according to United Nations policy. My experience has been exceptional and exciting, and it has drawn me towards the goal of using both legal and engineering knowledge to advance environmental regulation.

The fusion of engineering and law can be utilized to impact every facet of American society, and I plan to use my engineering knowledge and experience, coupled with the legal expertise I expect to gain at Fordham University Law School, first to help corporations to comply with existing environmental law effectively and efficiently; and then to develop advanced environmental regulations for local, regional and national agencies. Community regulations should be updated to consider those who must comply with regulations and those who must enforce the law. With a specialization in environmental law, I would be able to use my engineering skills to aid the legal field, investigating and developing environmental regulations for the demands of the new millennium. To that end, I am looking forward to working in environmental advocacy through the Fordham's Public Interest Resource Center. Applying my knowledge of environmental law while representing clients in actual cases will allow me experience and understanding that I could not gain anywhere else. The education that I would receive while helping others, as well as from the Fordham Law School faculty, would enable me to achieve all of my goals.

Anonymous

Anonymous was a double major in government & politics and sociology. He was active on campus and received several awards for outstanding leadership in campus organizations. He paid for 100 percent of his college expenses by founding an Internet publishing company and received national media attention for his sites. Professionally, he interned in the U.S. Senate and published several papers on African American policy issues while interning at one of the nation's premier minority think tanks.

Stats:

LSAT: 151, 158
GPA: 3.48 (government/politics and sociology)
College attended: University of Maryland—College Park
Class: 2001
Hometown: Pittsburgh, PA ("although I lived in Maryland full-time for five years and my applications reflected that")
Gender: Male
Race: White
Law school attending: The George Washington University Law School
Class: 2005

Applied to the following law schools:

Accepted: George Washington University, University of Maryland
Denied: Georgetown
Other: None

Personal statement:

According to Anonymous, "For GW the directions were as follows: 'All applicants are required to submit a personal statement which should include any additional information you think might be of assistance to the Admissions Committee in considering your application. Examples of such information are

significant extracurricular or community activities, the reasons why you want to study law, a discussion of your background, or an explanation of any unusual aspects of your academic record. This statement must be written on separate pages and must accompany this application.' Maryland's and Georgetown's were quite similar."

As applications from hopeful law school applicants roll into admissions offices this season, it is clear that admissions decisions will be as competitive as ever. Those applicants who are able to define themselves as disciplined, focused, serious, and excited about their future legal education will likely find success. I believe that I am one such candidate, and I believe that my unique background, academic and professional experiences, and personal drive define me as a candidate that will be a strong addition to The George Washington Law School.

My decision to apply to law schools followed a different route than most. After attending a wealthier high school that was racially and socially homogenous in the suburbs of Pittsburgh, Pennsylvania, I felt that I was missing out on the "real world." It was difficult for me to shake the feeling that I wasn't truly experiencing the diversity of the nation and the peoples and cultures within it. I decided to move to and attend school near Washington, DC, where I felt I could further my interest in different cultures as well as get hands on opportunities in government and politics and social issues, my major choices of study.

In hindsight, I believe that my decision to move to the area was the right one, and my undergraduate years were times of further discovery personally, academically, and professionally. Money was often a problem for my family, and while both of my divorced parents made every effort to help me financially, more often than not it was up to me. I fully supported myself throughout my undergraduate years, primarily through the founding of my own Internet publishing business. While I was fortunate to have been able to work in such a flexible way, the work was not easy. There was a high level of complexity and volatility in the infant industry at the time. I was forced to learn the ever-changing laws and regulations "on the fly," and my dealings with contract, tax, copyright, and intellectual property law helped me to begin to realize the extraordinary value of a formal legal education.

The fact that I needed to support myself was never one that I took lightly. I am completely financially independent, and there were always tough decisions to be made, especially when others around me had no such restrictions. The income from the business fluctuated greatly, and I was constantly faced with tough questions. Can I afford to take the LSAT test-prep course? How much rent can I afford per month? How will this financial choice affect my future ability to pay for school? There were many difficult decisions to make, but living with such restrictions, financial and otherwise, allowed me to gain a personal discipline that served me well in other aspects of my life.

My strong preparation for a formal legal education is further demonstrated in my ideologically diversified work experience. I worked at one of the most liberal think tanks in America studying African American political issues, and I also worked in the Senate office of one of the most conservative Senators on the Hill, Pat Roberts of Kansas. I served as a "tester" for a major civil rights firm by entering places of business to compare how I was treated as a customer compared to how clients of the firm reported that they were treated. I have also published two articles regarding minority political participation, one of which was presented to the NAACP in Baltimore, MD. All of these experiences helped me to realize that taking an approach that respects and appreciates different points of view is imperative. This is a realization that I constantly keep in mind in my day-to-day dealings, and one that I feel will serve me well as I further my education.

While at George Washington University Law School, I plan to continue to follow my interests in public service and social issues. I am especially excited about the institution's Public Interest Law Scholars Program. I believe that applying the knowledge that an individual has attained in a leadership setting is one of the most gratifying and valuable acts in which one can partake. I have aspirations of becoming a public figure or elected official in the areas of civil rights and constitutional law, and I believe the well-rounded legal education that The George Washington University Law School would provide me would be integral in my efforts to achieve these goals.

Certainly, there are many motivated and qualified candidates applying to law schools this year. However, I believe that the most successful students will be those who have clearly considered their life path, have practical experience, and are focused on their future legal education. I believe that my unique personal experiences, diverse professional background, strong academic record, and many leadership roles will give me an edge in a challenging educational environment. For these reasons, I believe that I should be carefully considered for admission to The George Washington University Law School.

Brian Frye

For several years Brian worked as a journalist, film curator, and artist. He has written feature articles and reviews for magazines including The New Republic, Film Comment, University Business, Civilization, *and* Independent Film and Video Monthly. *In addition to co-curating The Robert Beck Memorial Cinema, New York City's only weekly experimental film series, for four years, he has acted as curator of film programs at institutions including the Museum of Modern Art, the Whitney Museum of American Art, Pacific Film Archive, PS1, and Anthology Film Archives. Brian was one of 140 artists featured in the 2002 Whitney Biennial, and his films are shown frequently by museums and festivals around the world.*

Stats:

LSAT: 174

GPA: 3.6

College attended: University of California—Berkeley (film studies)

Class: 1995

Hometown: San Francisco, CA

Gender: Male

Race: White

Law school attending: Georgetown University Law Center

Class: 2005

Applied to the following law schools:
Accepted: Boston College, Georgetown, Tulane, University of Wisconsin—Madison, Washington & Lee
Denied: Harvard, University of California—Berkeley (Boalt)
Other: Columbia, Cornell, University of Virginia (placed on waitlist by all)

Personal statement:
In Brian's words, his statement "was not written in response to any particular question."

Some time ago, I encountered a charming - though quite possibly apocryphal - anecdote concerning the lawyer and poet Wallace Stevens. Supposedly, Stevens composed his poems in the morning while walking to his office, where he dictated them to his secretary for transcription. As the law cleaves to the Socratic method, his poetry apparently found its nourishment in the Peripatetics.

In Stevens's seamless integration of art and the law, I found a poetically ironic model for myself. Though Stevens's vocation and his avocation were quite distinct, they nonetheless complemented one another, metaphorically and otherwise. For almost ten years, I have devoted myself to the study and practice of film as a fine art. I do not intend to abandon it. I can only hope to strike a balance between art and the law so effortless and natural.

Fortunately, there is every reason to believe it possible. The law has long maintained a closer affinity to the arts than many might admit. Oliver Wendell Holmes - possibly the greatest Chief Justice of the Supreme Court - was a friend of literature, and even wrote sonnets as a young soldier. When he took up the study of law, it was with some trepidation, tempered by a deep belief in the richness of its dusty verities. As he put it, "law is human - it is a part of man, and of one world with all the rest."

My longstanding interest in studying law crystallized while reading Holmes. I found myself both broadly in agreement with his description of the law, and deeply sympathetic to his conception of the proper role of its practitioners. Holmes held that a man's highest duty lay in the assiduous performance of his professional responsibilities, the perquisite to "strive for the superlative."

An oft-wounded veteran of the Civil War, Holmes knew of the passions excited by convictions strongly held, and mistrusted their claim to truth. He brought to the law a rare, pragmatic humility and deference to historical experience, an understanding that the soul of our Constitution rests in the ability of its core principles to respond to history of their own accord, with a minimum of coercion.

In his dissent to Abrams v. United States, Justice Holmes described our Constitution as, "an experiment, as all life is an experiment." Consequently, he advocated a broader, more permissive reading of the amendment than previously known, in the expectation that the freest market in ideas should likely furnish the soundest ones. Significantly, Holmes argued not for an abstract and immutable freedom to say whatever one likes, but rather a staying of the still-reserved power to suppress that proven seditious.

I believe that lawyers are something like the laboratory scientists of the public sphere. While legislators create the law, the legal system shapes and makes sense of it. Lawyers address themselves to the law as it stands, rather than asking how it might otherwise be. Just as one doesn't fashion grand new theories in the laboratory, one doesn't write law in the courtroom. It is in the crucible of the laboratory, however, that the failings of an apparently plausible theory become apparent. I want very much to become one of those experimenters in the courtroom.

Until recently, it had become merely fashionable to proclaim the novelty of today's world. Suddenly, that claim has acquired a gravity none expected, and we must shoulder grave responsibilities none imagined. I believe that the demands placed by both commerce and justice on the law will, of necessity, reflect our changed world. But the problems and questions posed will not be solved by fiat. Rather, it will be by that familiar, slow process of accretion and inflection that the law will find expression. I hope to do whatever I am able to assist that process.

Edmund Wilson wrote of Holmes's "conviction that the United States has a special meaning and mission to devote one's life to, which was a sufficient dedication for the highest gifts." I can only agree. And if the great experiment that is our Constitution sufficed for one so great as Holmes, it is all the more ample for those of more modest gifts, such as myself.

Emily Woodward

Emily was an English major at the College of William and Mary, where she graduated summa cum laude. During her junior and senior years, she worked as an off-site communications intern for NASA's Stennis Space Center. Following graduation, she worked as an online reporter for Defense News and a weekend producer for www.WashingtonPost.com. She looks forward to continuing both jobs while attending Georgetown University Law Center's evening program.

Stats:
LSAT: 165
GPA: 3.86
College attended: College of William and Mary
Class: 2000
Hometown: Alexandria, VA
Gender: Female
Race: White
Law school attending: Georgetown University Law Center
Class: 2006

Applied to the following law schools:
Accepted: Chicago-Kent College of Law, George Mason, Georgetown (evening program)
Denied: None
Other: None

Personal statement:
(For Georgetown)

"Last year, Georgetown received over 11,000 applications for the 450 full-time and 125 part-time first-year places. Most of these applicants are capable of successfully completing a Georgetown legal education. Because we cannot accept all qualified applicants, we have found statements to be valuable in the selection process. You may write your personal statement on any subject of importance to you that you feel will assist us in our decision."

Statement of Purpose

My desire to apply to law school is not rooted in a childhood fantasy of arguing a case before a packed courtroom. I have never seen myself as trial attorney ala Perry Mason or Nora Lewin on *Law & Order*. However, I have come to recognize a legal education would enable me to advance in my career as a writer and analyst specializing in national security and global trade issues.

I first set my sights on becoming a writer around the time I learned my letters. Of course, mastering the ABC's may have been a long way from winning the Pulitzer. This minor detail did not prevent me, however, from completing three "novels" and my own version of Genesis before the age of seven. Throughout elementary and junior high school, I annoyed my teachers by writing 10-page themes whenever they asked for a few sentences. Later, as a high school and college student, I continued writing, though my attention was increasingly turned toward other subjects.

While attending Thomas Jefferson High School for Science and Technology in Alexandria, Virginia, I immersed myself in biology, chemistry, and physics. Although I dreamed of being a professional author or journalist, I had grown convinced that I needed a science background to succeed in an increasingly high-tech world. This belief stayed with me after I headed south to Williamsburg, Virginia, to attend the College of William and Mary. Only after spending my freshman and sophomore years as Chemistry major – pouring over red-band spectral signatures and inhaling sulfurous concoctions in lab – did I finally accept the fact that I was no Marie Curie. Indeed, I realized I would have to spend all my waking hours just to make it as a mediocre chemist. Still, I wasn't comfortable switching to the Humanities (perhaps as a result of my laborious study of inertia in Physics 102). My wariness ebbed, however, in the wake of an even greater change in my college plans.

In the summer of 1998, I underwent surgery, which precluded my return to William and Mary in the Fall. Fortunately, I was able to take classes as an Extended Studies student at George Mason University, while wrapping up my period of convalescence at my home in Alexandria. The change of scenery inspired me to pursue new fields of study. I started taking courses in Shakespeare, Modern American Drama, Public Policy and Middle Eastern History. At the same time, I continued studying Chemistry and Biology, though I no longer wished to concentrate in the hard sciences.

Ultimately, one of my George Mason professors directed me on a path that would combine my background in science and technology background with my love of writing and my new interests in government and policymaking. With her help, I secured an internship with an Annandale, Virginia-based government contractor. I spent the spring and summer of 1999 writing copy for Web sites the company managed for NASA and the Department of Energy, while taking additional classes at George Mason and George Washington University.

I returned to William in Mary in the autumn of 1999 and completed my degree in English. I then went back to work briefly as a copywriter for the Annandale contracting firm. In February 2000, I accepted a job as a researcher at *Defense News,* a publication in suburban Washington, D.C., where I am now an assistant editor.

My current job entails researching and reporting on defense appropriations bills and export legislation, as well as writing daily summaries of major contracts awarded by the Department of Defense and other defense ministries worldwide. It is with enthusiasm, but some degree of trepidation, that I attempt to decode pages of legal jargon for an educated lay readership, many of which I suspect know more than I about such policies. Too often, I find I lack the legal knowledge to fully grasp bills that control how U.S. companies do business overseas, the limits to which federal agencies can go to collect covert intelligence, or the amount of funding an agency can receive in a given length of time.

On one hand, these limitations have done little to impair me in my current position, in which I am called to turn out several short stories each day on a variety of topics without going into significant detail. However, I would like to advance to more difficult reporting assignments one day. I fear I will be unable to do so without acquiring more expertise than I can obtain within the confines of my deadline-driven job. I also would like to It is a belief shared by several of my colleagues, as well as many of the senior writers and editors at my company who hold advanced degrees in law, business and related disciplines. I feel that a law degree would put me in a better position to join their ranks, particularly if I could attend school while continuing to work as a journalist.

Given my circumstances and interests, Georgetown University Law Center, with its top-ranked programs in intellectual property and international law, is my ideal choice. I have a colleague that is currently enrolled in the Georgetown evening law program. His generous feedback has helped convince me that this program also would fit my needs, in light of its flexible schedule and its emphasis on legal writing.

Anonymous

Anonymous was heavily involved in college government, especially during her junior year, when she managed the student activity fee and oversaw the funding and accounts of all student organizations on campus. She was a member of several significant committees on campus, including the cabinet of college government and the budget advisory committee of the college, and supervised the work of three student employees. She also had a show on the campus radio station and worked with a group whose mission was to free the campus bookstore of sweatshop-produced goods. She spent two summers interning in the marketing department of a large Boston law firm and worked as a teaching assistant, grader, and tutor in the math department at Wellesley during the fall of her senior year.

Stats:

LSAT: 167

GPA: 3.85 (math and psychology)

College attended: Wellesley College

Class: 2002

Hometown: Whitman, MA

Gender: Female

Race: White

Law school attending: Harvard Law School

Class: 2005

Applied to the following law schools:

Accepted: Boston College, Boston University, Cornell, Georgetown, Harvard, NYU

Denied: None

Other: Columbia (placed on reserve; Anonymous withdrew her application)

Personal statement:

Anonymous did not write her personal statement in response to any particular question.

It's two in the morning, and I'm taking a break from working on my Analysis problem set. Theorems have been swimming around my head, bumping into each other, and sometimes (thankfully) connecting, for the past four hours. Although I have a hard time admitting it to myself (can I really be that much of a math dork?), I'm in my element. It's times like this that make me feel like I have some sort of deeper understanding of the world around me. Like the blue print of existence, math is everywhere, and it is consistent. Propositions, functions, dimensions and limits – all of math, really - fit together like the most elegantly constructed puzzle imaginable. When you're in the middle of it, it's almost intoxicating in it's beauty.

Logic is the glue that holds the pieces of the mathematical puzzle together, and it is the reason that the puzzle pieces fit together so well. Similarly, logic is at the heart of legal reasoning. But the law has something more to it than that—the law is fundamentally human. While math exists outside the realm of the mind, law comes from the heart of the human soul. It is the set of rules that we, as a species, have created so that we can maximize our interactions with one another and improve our experiences on this earth. Consequently, I view the law as the common ground of math and psychology, and although I may get strange looks when I tell people that I'm a math and psych double major headed to law school, it all makes perfect sense to me.

The relationship between math, psychology, and law isn't the only reason I want to make my life in the law. Ideally, law improves the lives of those it encompasses, and it is noble in that respect. Maybe it's youthful optimism, but I'd like to think that when I die, the world will be a better place for having had me in it. In high school, I volunteered for a non-profit organization that focused on educating and supporting teenaged mothers. I've always remembered the night that I overheard Jill, one of the mothers whom I'd gotten to know quite well, crying on the phone to her daughter's father. Their baby was sick with a bad cold, and Jill didn't have enough money to buy her medicine, I was struck by how unfair it was that although Jill and I were the same age, and lived within a few miles of each other, our lives were worlds apart. I knew then that I couldn't single-handedly tackle all of the inequalities in American society, but that night I promised myself that whatever career I chose, I would work to level the playing field as much as I could.

Evil lawyer jokes aside, the law is perhaps the most powerful mechanism for both large and small-scale social improvements, and that is the real reason why I have chosen to enter the field. As much as I love math, I know that contemplating the magic of Fourier series isn't going to make the world a better place. You can't feed a hungry child with ternary expansion, or provide housing to low-income elderly with Lebesgue integration. Psychology does have the potential to improve human life, but it lacks the logical foundation shared by math and law. Thus while math and psychology aren't without merit, I don't want to spend my life with either subject.

I'm not sure where I'll be in ten years. I've already spent two summers working for a large, corporate law firm. The experience was valuable because it taught me a lot about the law in general, but I know that sort of practice isn't for me. Maybe I'll work for a non-profit like the one I used to volunteer for. Maybe I'll be involved in government, helping to make public policy decisions. Maybe I'll be on my way to becoming a judge on the Federal circuit. The possibilities are endless, and I don't really have a master plan. I do know, though, that law is a natural choice for me. Whatever I do with it, because of the promise I made to myself years ago, I'll fall asleep each night knowing that someone out there is better off because of the work I did that day.

Anonymous

Anonymous graduated magna cum laude from the University of Notre Dame with a B.A. in government and a minor in international peace studies. She was the recipient of a Lilly Foundation Community Scholarship, a four-year, full-tuition award. Anonymous has been on the Dean's List for eight semesters and is a four-time University Scholar. An avid government major, she was recently inducted into Pi Sigma Alpha, a government honor society, and interned for Phil Hope, MP in the British House of Commons, in 2000. Anonymous is a 2001 Truman Scholar for the state of Indiana. She has worked for the past five summers at the Allen County Public Defender's Office as an investigator and court liaison.

Stats:

LSAT: Anonymous wished not to disclose her LSAT scores.
GPA: 3.75 (government)
College attended: University of Notre Dame
Class: 2002
Hometown: Fort Wayne, IN
Gender: Female
Race: Anonymous wished not to disclose her race.
Law school attending: Harvard Law School
Class: 2005

Applied to the following law schools:

Accepted: Chicago-Kent, College of William and Mary, Harvard, Indiana University, Loyola University of Chicago, Northwestern, University of Pennsylvania
Denied: Yale
Other: University of Virginia (placed on waitlist)

Personal statement:

Anonymous did not write her personal statement in response to any particular question.

I prefer the blues to Pavarotti. I'd take Shakespeare over Dickens any day. I hate red nail polish and I love to vacuum. I've played the clarinet for 15 years. I've played the saxophone for 10. I watch cartoons on Saturday mornings. *The Catcher in the Rye* is my favorite novel. I seem to have a propensity for the challenging. And I like it.

***

My mom and I lived in a rented house on the South side of town. I was often left alone in the early years of my life – left to cook for myself, to watch late night t.v. and left to answer the door when strange people knocked just after midnight. My maternal grandparents did what they could and picked me up once a week to give me a bath, often my only for the week, and to take me out to dinner. Other times, they sent over plates of food and packets of vitamins for me. My mom ate the food and tried to sell the vitamins for drugs.

Meanwhile, as I waited for my grandparents to pick me up on our front porch, I was so hungry I ate the peeling paint.

I saw my first gun Christmas Eve, 1989. Mom was afraid Big Bird was chasing her. When this happened, my grandparents looked at each other with worried eyes and said the drugs were talking again.

I don't remember what I got for Christmas that year.

My grandparents have had custody of me since I was 4 and they legally adopted me when I was 11, just after my mother's suicide. For the past 18 years, my grandparents have raised me, and run their household, on social security. But they never let me think of myself as poor or underprivileged – as a result I capitalized on the opportunities made available to me. Now that I am a university student, my grandparents have cashed in their retirement savings to continue to raise and have given their livelihood to shape mine.

I spent the last summer trying to preserve my grandmother's.

Every day this past summer I had a standing date at seven in the morning and night with my grandma to help her take her pills because she couldn't remember how. In the mornings before work I would spend an additional 20 minutes practicing picking up the phone with her and reminding her how to speak into it so she could talk to me when I called.

By mid-September that morning and evening date had turned into a date at the nursing home every weekend.

Instead of learning how the phone worked, she had me feel her face to make sure it was still there.

Thanksgiving day 2001 started out like any other and after dinner at a neighbor's house my grandfather and I went to visit grandma. I remember that her eyes were bluer than I'd ever seen and her breath like that of a fish out of water. And for the next 45 minutes my grandmother communicated to me through her eyes what her mouth could not – how our souls were connected and how she'd loved me before I was born.

At 8pm that Thanksgiving day, with her lungs full of water and her heart too tired to beat, my grandma passed from this world to the next.

***

I spend 10 minutes a day making my bed. I love horror movies and am in a continual quest to find the scariest movie. I enjoy reading Habermasian discourse of communicative action. I always, without fail, microwave my lunch too long. I listened to my first Ella Fitzgerald CD a week before she died. I haven't stopped listening since. I like delis. I appreciate my professors.

***

It's dominated my life for the past four and a half years. Because of it, my collection of suits has exponentially increased. It inexplicably pops up in a majority of my conversations.

My work at the Public Defender's Office has seen me do everything from prepare for daily arraignments, spend afternoons in the county jail advising our clients, liaison with various local, state and national agencies, interview witnesses for murder cases and substantiate defense alibis for use at trial. As an investigator and court liaison for the PD's office since I was 18, I have been able to interact with a colorful cross-section of the Ft. Wayne community – interactions that have helped me realize that there is more to our clients than just their reason for being incarcerated. After four summers, I can say with pride that I spent my summers "in and out of jail". And, four summers later, I'm addressed as 'public-defender girl' or 'Miss ——' and stopped by former clients on the street so they can tell me how their probation is going or how their son started in his first Little League game the afternoon before. Through the Public Defender's office, I've found something I know I will be quite comfortable doing for the rest of my life.

At 22 now, I've come into my own...as a student of Notre Dame, of political theory, as a student of society and, as a Truman scholar, I've been given license and affirmation to do what I love best and become a public defender myself. That's why, instead of fleeing to an ivory tower, I am choosing to work in what some may call the trenches.

To me, it rings of a somewhat comfortable familiarity – I am but little removed from those I wish to help.

Michael Giordano

Michael majored in PPE (philosophy, politics & economics) at Pomona and served for four years on the college's Judiciary Council. He spent the fall of his junior year abroad at University College, Oxford, where he rowed crew poorly and studied occasionally. Pomona awarded him distinction on his senior thesis, a revised version of which was subsequently published in the UCLA Entertainment Law Review. After graduating cum laude, Michael bought himself another year of Southern California sunshine by deferring his Harvard Law School admission. He felt fortunate to be offered a position at the William Morris Agency—the world's oldest and largest talent and literary agency—where he worked for and learned from a vice president who also happened to be a lawyer.

Stats:
LSAT: 165, 166
GPA: 3.76
College attended: Pomona College
Class: 2001
Hometown: Walnut Creek, CA
Gender: Male
Race: White (Italian American)
Law school attending: Harvard Law School
Class: 2005

Applied to the following law schools:
Accepted: Duke (with large scholarship), Harvard, University of California—Los Angeles, University of Michigan
Denied: Stanford, Yale
Other: As Michael called them, "Non-decisions (waitlist, hold, etc.)": Columbia, NYU, University of California—Berkeley (Boalt), University of Chicago. Michael withdrew his application from each of these schools before any of them provided him with a final admission decision.

Personal statement:

(From Harvard Law School's Application for Admission)

"Applicants present themselves, their backgrounds, experiences, and ideas to the Admissions Committee in a Personal Statement. Because people and their experiences are diverse, you are the best person to determine the content of your own statement. It is for you to decide what information you would like to convey, and the best way for you to convey it. Whatever you write about, readers will be seeking to get a sense of you as a person and as a potential student and graduate of Harvard Law School. In this context, it is generally more helpful to write what you think readers should know to have a better sense of who you are rather than writing what you think the readers want to read.

"The Personal Statement can be an opportunity to illuminate your intellectual background and interests, or to provide information about yourself and your achievements that may not be fully evident through other information provided in the application. In many ways, you are preparing a case. As in most legal cases, it is important to be persuasive, clear, succinct, and timely. There are few substitutes for careful forethought and planning in this process.

"We understand that it can be difficult to discuss oneself on paper, but our experience is that written statements are valuable in the selection process. Candid, forthright and thoughtful statements are always the most helpful."

Ninety-nine-point-nine percent.

"That's what they told me," "Sebastian" mumbled, unsure of himself. A black man who looked too young to get into a bar and sounded too naive to try, Sebastian came off as simple and innocent. But this father of four was nowhere near as young as he appeared. And according to the police, he was nowhere near as innocent either.

Sebastian was charged with first-degree murder, and he faced the possibility of a life sentence with no parole. Though inadmissible in court, his polygraph results were disheartening. They indicated that the chances were 999 in 1000 that he had not told the whole truth. I began to wonder whether I had been misguided when I boarded a plane for Washington, D.C. — with no place to stay and not enough money to afford the few places I would find — hoping to pursue justice.

A few months earlier, in the wake of an inspiring social and political philosophy class that had challenged me to redefine and then defend my conception of justice, I found myself swamped with applications for summer internships. Hoping to challenge myself while exploring the relationship between justice and fairness, I submitted an application to the Criminal Law Internship Program at the Public Defender Service for the District of Columbia. I felt fortunate to be offered a position as an intern investigator and case assistant.

After two weeks of intensive training, I was assigned to Rudy *****, the PDS Training Director who handled only first-degree felonies. Rudy's cases became my life, Sebastian my primary concern. Most days I would arrive at Rudy's office before he did, a bit worn out by my long commute from an economically depressed Maryland suburb, but interested in reviewing what I had done the previous day. In the midst of investigating other cases, it took me a week to locate Sebastian and another few days to complete an interview with him. Unfortunately, the friends whose names Sebastian had given me refused to answer my questions because the police had told them not to communicate with me.

Frustrated by the way in which the police had apparently tried to obstruct justice, I visited the crime scene in an attempt to determine the accuracy of their incident report. I noticed immediately that the eyewitness' window, obscured by large trees, would not have allowed him to view the entire altercation. Furthermore, the great distance between the window and the crime scene, coupled with the broken streetlight nearby, implied that a positive facial identification in the middle of the night would have been virtually impossible. How could the police have missed this crucial information?

The police probably did not miss anything, as they sought only corroborating evidence. I realized at this point that the scales of justice weighed heavily against Sebastian even before his trial began. While the well-funded U.S. Attorney's Office had an entire police force working toward Sebastian's conviction, PDS could hardly pay its hardworking lawyers a living wage, let alone hire enough trained investigators to counterbalance the police. Despite this realization, I continued to investigate the case, hoping to bolster Rudy's arguments demonstrating Sebastian's innocence.

Before the court set a trial date, summer drew to a close. I was disappointed that I would not be able to testify on Sebastian's behalf. My work led me to conclude that, while Sebastian may not have been entirely guiltless, he definitely was not guilty of first-degree murder. The eyewitness had mistakenly identified Sebastian as the perpetrator.

Shortly after I had returned to California, I received a call from Rudy. "We won the case — Sebastian's free!" Justice had prevailed. Frankly, I was surprised, albeit pleasantly, to hear that a seemingly unfair justice system had produced a just outcome. Then it hit me. Working within a system that gave the prosecution a head start, Rudy came from behind to win freedom for Sebastian. Justice prevailed only because of Rudy's efforts to overcome the disadvantages with which the system had saddled Sebastian.

Rudy's handling of Sebastian's case taught me that the conception of justice I had come to defend in my philosophy class is attainable even when the system seems to favor the prosecution. But it requires that a dedicated and well-trained defense attorney make up the lost ground. Because I believe in defending my conception of justice beyond the confines of a classroom, I want to attend law school so that I may follow in Rudy's footsteps. I only hope that I will be able to make up as much ground for my clients as Rudy did for Sebastian.

The last time I communicated with Rudy, I explained that working with him had marked a turning point in my life. Armed with a clearer sense of my goals, I returned to my studies more motivated and interested than I had ever been, and I received the best grades of my life last fall at Oxford and last spring at Pomona. After hearing this, Rudy asked what the chances were that I would be attending law school.

"Honestly? About ninety-nine-point-nine percent."

Ryan Spear

As an undergraduate, Ryan served as a research assistant, tutor, and mentor. He later edited a literary journal and a newspaper for immigrants, refugees, and low-income people.

Stats:

LSAT: 170

GPA: 3.85; master's degree, 4.0

College attended: University of Washington (literature); master's degree from Portland State University (literature)

Class: 1997; master's degree, 2000

Hometown: Vancouver, WA

Gender: Male

Race: White

Law school attending: Harvard Law School

Class: 2006

Applied to the following law schools:

Accepted: Harvard, Stanford

Denied: None

Other: None

Personal statement:

(For Harvard)

"Please present yourself, your background and experiences, and your ideas as you wish in a brief personal statement.

"To provide a context for writing your statement, we offer the following observations. The personal statement can be an opportunity to illuminate your intellectual background and interests. You might do this by writing about a course, academic project, book, artistic or cultural experience that has been important to you. The personal statement can also be an opportunity to clarify or elaborate on other information that you have provided in the application and to provide information about yourself and your achievements that may not be evident to the readers of your application. Because people and their experiences are diverse, you are the best person to determine the content of your own statement. It is for you to decide what information you would like to convey and the best way for you to convey it. Whatever you write about, readers of your statement will be seeking to get a sense of you as a person and as a potential student and graduate of Harvard Law School."

(For Stanford)

"Enclose a statement of about two pages describing important or unusual aspects of yourself not otherwise apparent in your application.

"While admission to Stanford Law School is based primarily upon superior academic achievement and potential to contribute to the legal profession, the Admissions Committee also regards the diversity of an entering class as important to the School's educational mission. If you would like the committee to consider how factors such as your background, life and work experiences, advanced studies, extracurricular or community activities, culture, class, race, or ethnicity would contribute to the diversity of the entering class and hence to your classmates' law school experience, please describe these factors and their relevance."

My first rushes of intellectual excitement were not literary or scientific; they were inspired by principles and procedure. I distinctly remember my mind awakening to itself on two occasions: while writing bills at Boys State and, later, while drafting examinations for our high school mock trial team. Neither of these experiences were revelatory. I was not, that young, inflamed with the idea that law school was my One True Destiny. But immature as I was, I could already sense that there was something recognizably right about this type of work.

No surprise, then, that as an undergraduate I spent much of my time at the intersection of people and rules. As a resident adviser, orientation coordinator and instructor, I found that I was good at helping people relate to and navigate institutions. In my academic life, meanwhile, I was discovering a love of variety. I found that the sharper my facility with words and ideas became, the more sophisticatedly I could think about arguments occurring in other fields: ecology, physiology, physics. By the time I left the University of Washington, I understood that I was at my best and happiest wrestling with problems (environmental law, for example, or educational policy) that required a multi-disciplinary perspective and diplomatic bent.

Looking to mobilize that insight against more life-and-death sorts of problems, I gave a year of service to AmeriCorps. As a volunteer coordinator, I gained valuable experience in negotiation and community building. Perhaps more valuably, I ran up against many of the sobering realities of professional activism – partisanship, bureau-cracy, the limits of my own patience – before I was able to over-romanticize that rôle.

Graduate school confirmed that purely aesthetic work couldn't satisfy me. I loved editing the Portland Review, but I did not love the feeling of irrelevance that often crept in while editing copy or selling a revision. Meanwhile, in the classroom, I was becoming a far more able critic of bad thinking. A voice at my shoulder (Stanley Fish, I now think) encouraged me to connect that ability to more practical issues.

Thus my editorship of The Voice, King County's newspaper for immigrants, refugees and low-income people. At The Voice, I've been able to disentangle the intricacies of HOPE VI redevelopment, publicize the human costs of welfare reform and ferret out anti-Muslim backlash after Sept. 11. This is a great job: fascinating and instructive. But it is also fundamentally observational and eccentric, and if I've learned anything about my mind, it is its preference for direct contact. I just wasn't meant to be a reporter, quite frankly.

So why sprint through all this? My story lacks an essay-ready burning bush moment, and its (admittedly inelegant) variety resists sweeping themes. But my intellectual and professional progress is relevant because it has been an education in the root sense of the word: a wide-ranging "leading out" from vague yearnings for an intellectually challenging, problem-oriented career to a mature understand-ing of why I want to attend law school. This is not to over-idealize the profession or my decision; I don't expect the law to harmonize the legislator, the academic, the activist and the editor in me. After all, to harmonize those impulses might be to neutralize them, and I intend to deploy them all at [school].

No, I'm not excited about a legal education because it promises some sort of intellectual nirvana, but because all my research suggests it demands and rewards much of what I've gained over the years: intellectual rigor, imagination and a love of learning (to name a few). More importantly, I believe a legal career will allow me to apply what I've learned – powerfully and directly – to a vast constellation of current and still unimaginable problems. Simply put, in [school] I see an education that marries my need to think with my need to do; a career that satisfies my desire to get at the guts of complicated problems; not an apocalyptic fulfillment of but the next chapter in my search for the best, most meaningful work.

Shane Shelley

Shane studied English literature and sociology at Stanford University, receiving a B.A. and an M.A., respectively. He has traveled throughout Europe and Morocco and spent a single academic term at Oxford University. During college, Shane supported himself with odd jobs, including waiting tables, publishing, and sociological research. Currently, he tutors and teaches part time.

Stats:

LSAT: 175
GPA: 3.72 (English literature)
College attended: Stanford University
Class: 2001
Hometown: San Diego, CA
Gender: Male
Race: White
Law school attending: Harvard Law School
Class: 2005

Applied to the following law schools:

Accepted: Columbia, Duke, Georgetown, Harvard, NYU, University of California—Berkeley (Boalt), University of Michigan, University of San Diego, University of Virginia
Denied: Stanford, Yale
Other: None

Personal statement:

In Shane's words, "The question that prompted my statement, namely the one from Harvard, generally just asked for a couple-page statement about anything you would like to discuss."

In personal statements, we often struggle to convey exalted intentions, as though that could reveal our virtuous nature, or any nature really, in these several pages. A German philosopher wrote that because we have only one life, we can never know whether we have made the best decisions on our path. No one can honestly say what he should or should not do, nor what he should or should not have done; he can only say, and even then with little assurance, what he will or will not do. With this knowledge, according to the philosopher, I could not, in good faith, express an intention in this statement, having no knowledge of the outcome of any decision. This past summer I composed the following passage, based on an earlier experience in the Moroccan wilderness. Reading over the passage, I have found the excerpt aptly applies to a discussion of intention within this context:

"He kneeled at the side of the river and stared at his reflection; a bearded man stared back. As he dipped his hands into the brown waters his arms disappeared beneath the surface. He shook his arms in the water, cleaning them, and then gathered some in his hands and splashed his face. He looked again and now the reflection rippled, fragmented by the movement of the brown water. He could not see into the depths of the river and only saw the strange and fragmented face of the bearded man; he wondered if he knew himself at all.

The face of a large steer appeared before him in the reflection. The steer shook its head in the heat and he could feel its breath on his back. The steer seemed alone. He turned around and saw a small boy at the side of the steer hauling a cart of potatoes. The small boy led the steer to the riverside with a long reed switch. The sun was behind them, above the canyon edge and the waterfall, and cast the boy and steer in dark shadows; he could not see the face of the small boy, but he heard his shouted commands in the Berber language."

The assumption of intention presupposes that in some dark corner of our souls a causal force, free from the determinism of an indifferent world, forms the ground of an intentional act. Such a force runs as a dense and clouded river through the heart, much as the river described above. The river reflects everything of my being—appearance, demeanor, ideology, decisions made—and yet, when I plunge my arms into its murky depths, even they disappear in the obscurity. The river of an intentional soul remains concealed from its very possessor.

The waters of the river, however, are seasonal, and become clear in the fall. With winter comes death; I must wait, then, until the eve of my demise for the illumination of that dark corner. But out of desperate impatience I thrash with my arms the murky waters, shaking them into a momentary clarity. Cupping the clear waters on the surface into my hands, I raise the lucid pool from the brown river. The actual intention, the outward manifestation of a conscious decision, forms in the moment before the moment, the reflection disturbed to reveal another much the same but later in the day and changed, and a man forges himself and his intentions anew, thrashing almost indiscriminately, as best he can. Perhaps he has taken the proper course; perhaps no proper course exists; nevertheless he must try and disturb the waters, in an attempt to clear them for a moment and create new courses and new reasons for his being.

The short passage, written some time ago without any specific purpose, a naked and unsettled metaphor, becomes relevant through interpretation, an intention and meaning distilled from the murky waters of an obscure art and an opaque soul. This personal statement and the passage come to reflect the formless deluge of an intentional heart taking shape as outward intentions under the damming and distillation of my mind and its decisions. The thrashing about of an arm in the murky water becomes the decision to attend law school; and with the thrashing comes a new clarity in the river.

The study of law, from a humanist perspective taking law as a reflection of social development, could be viewed as the study of a gradual, groping realization of human potential, a potential inherent in every individual. Man realizes his human nature through an application of this vague potential—rather than a revelation of something already there—toward the creation of a human, social world, in this case a world founded on the formation of law. The philosopher may dismiss the presentation of intention as an impossible fiction, and at some level I might agree. But to the extent that something such as law creates a human truth for the world and our nature, I would like to do the same with myself, and create a personal truth through action and forged intentions, such as the action and intention of attending law school. That small boy was so young he could hardly understand why he drove the cart to and from the river, and yet he commanded a much larger steer with his reed switch. In my most honest moments, I see myself as that boy, trying, with everything he can stubbornly muster, to move a great world he only understands as important, wonderful, and somehow meaningful.

Amanda Motsinger

Amanda was a member of Delta Gamma sorority for all four years of college, and she held offices and volunteered many hours for its national philanthropy, Service for Sight. She also served as a campus legislator and events programmer for the two largest quadrangles on Duke's campus and swam on Duke's club swim team. Amanda worked as a teaching assistant for a computer science course for five semesters. After graduation she was employed for a year as a paralegal for a Wall Street law firm working predominantly on corporate liability law.

Stats:

LSAT: 174
GPA: 3.29 (economics)
College attended: Duke University
Class: 2001
Hometown: Winston-Salem, NC
Gender: Female
Race: White
Law school attending: New York University School of Law
Class: 2005

Applied to the following schools:

Accepted: Boston College, Benjamin M. Cardozo School of Law, Emory, Fordham, George Washington University, Georgetown, NYU, University of North Carolina—Chapel Hill

Denied: None

Other: Columbia, University of Pennsylvania, University of Virginia

Personal statement:

"The Committee on Admissions encourages you to provide any information that may be helpful to us in reaching a thoughtful decision on your application. While the choice as to whether or what information to submit to the Committee is entirely yours, any information you provide will be used to give you full credit for your accomplishments, to help the Committee reach an informed decision on your application, and to aid the Committee in selecting a diverse student body.

"Examples of information which have been useful in the past include descriptions or documentation of disabilities, an explicit history of standardized test results, unusual circumstances which may have affected academic performance, or personal/family history of educational or socioeconomic disadvantage. While this list is not all-inclusive, we offer it to you to think about as you consider whether such information might be relevant in your case, and to assure you that including it is quite appropriate."

The first time that I recall giving thought to the profession of law was during high school Latin class. I studied Latin during all four years of high school because it seemed more interesting than other languages as Latin involves not only the study of literature but also of history and mythology. I remember learning my freshman year that the second king of Rome, Numa Pompilius, was notable for giving the city its vaunted laws, thereby instituting order and civility in the area. Having lived in a law-abiding society all my life, I was very interested and a bit confused by this fact. How was it that a city existed without laws, and how does one bestow laws on a society? I had never given any thought to these questions, simply believing the laws of American society to be universal and unchangeable, but throughout the next four years of high school Latin, I learned as much as I could about the malleability of the laws of ancient Rome and the different processes by which the legal system operated under the monarchy, the republic, and the Empire. Latin class also taught me that the American legal system has many similarities with that of ancient Rome. While I enjoyed the literature and the mythology that dominated Latin class, the influence of ancient Romans on the modern legal system interested me the most.

In college, however, I majored in the eminently more practical field of economics, finding to my pleasure that economics was integrally tied to the legal system in ways that I found even more interesting. I focused on economics courses dealing with government and its influences, both positive and negative, on business, in America and internationally. In these classes, I learned how the actions of Microsoft were considered by some as anti-competitive and why airline mergers were blocked because of antitrust concerns, and I was excited to be able to explain these complexities to my family and friends. These courses helped me to refine my area of interest to the intersection between economics and law.

This interest has grown during my recent employment with D'Amato & Lynch, a Wall Street firm that handles securities cases for the world's largest insurers of directors, officers, and corporate liability. Through my paralegal work, I have learned a great deal about how concepts that I studied in my economics courses are rooted in the legal world. This position has cemented my desire to pursue a career in law.

Thus, at New York University School of Law, I hope to focus on business law. My primary interests at this point are antitrust and intellectual property, both of which I have studied briefly and hope to learn in more depth. I find these areas of law intriguing for their intricacies and ever-changing natures in the current economy, and I want to be a part of the legal system as it evolves to deal with new issues in antitrust and intellectual property. No longer the high school Latin student intent on learning about ancient Rome, I want to study legal questions that are changing the future of business in the city that is now the center of the world, New York.

Leslie M. Fenton

While in college, Leslie took a quarter-long leave of absence to work for the democratic campaign for the 2000 election season. She was a gender studies major and worked on extracurricular activities that pertained to her field of study.

Stats:

LSAT: 170

GPA: 3.7 (gender studies)

College attended: University of Chicago

Class: 2002

Hometown: Highland Park, IL

Gender: Female

Race: White

Law school attending: New York University School of Law

Class: 2005

Applied to the following law schools:

Accepted: Columbia, Northwestern, University of Michigan, Washington University in St. Louis

Denied: Harvard, University of California—Berkeley (Boalt), Yale

Other: None

Personal statment:

In Leslie's words, "I sent the same personal statement to each school as a general explanation of 'why I want to study the law.'"

My decision to dedicate my life to civil rights activism as a lawyer has been a years-long process. As a gender studies major and sometime activist, I have studied and participated in many forms of action directed at changing society. While observing various modes of civil rights activism, I came to realize that the most effective and permanent means of transforming social consciousness is through the law.

When I worked as a field coordinator for the Washington Coordinated Democratic Campaign, a group of anarchists staged an anti-Gore protest in our office.

While the initial group of protestors was small and focused, the protest soon became unruly and scattered. In the end, our office suffered significant damage and neither the press nor community members understood the protestors' goals. At first, I understood their right to protest, but I soon realized that their methods had done nothing to deliver their message. They stormed our office hoping to change Gore's policies on oil companies, but when they left, the only thing changed was the newly spray-painted exterior of our building.

I began to sympathize with the initial goal of those protestors, however, when I helped stage a protest of my own at the University of Chicago last year. A student organization, with the help of our tuition money, invited an infamously racist speaker to visit our campus. As soon as I heard about the event, I posted fliers and emails to try to unite student and community groups against the talk. Unfortunately, I found that uniting groups in one cause for one event is a tricky, dangerous process. Each group wanted control of the organizing process, and they fought amongst each other as to the methods and motivations of the protest itself. I spent hours writing emails and talking on the phone just trying to convince representatives from one socialist group that a rival socialist group would not try to dominate the protest.

When the protest finally happened, it was in many ways successful. Almost 300 people showed up to oppose the speaker, while less than 100 came to support him. Many newspapers covered the event, each with unsurprisingly mixed reactions. For a moment, people in the community and on campus became more aware of issues pertaining to race and that particular student group. Beyond this, however, I have yet to notice any sort of permanent shift in social consciousness on campus. My goal in organizing the protest was to raise awareness among my fellow students. Very few African-American students actually attend our school, and yet the student group felt comfortable inviting a speaker that lashes out at African-Americans. Almost a year later, sadly, there is no increased discussion of diversity issues on campus, no unease about the lack of tolerance shown by certain student groups. We made people at our school think about race for a day, but these thoughts were only temporary.

I understand that societal change, initiated legally or otherwise, is slow to occur.

One has to look generations beyond the actual law to realize that change has happened. I think the example that best speaks to my point is the landmark 1954 Supreme Court decision *Brown vs. the Board of Education*. While there are still people who agree with segregation, our society as a whole recognizes that black students have fundamental civil rights under the Constitution that would be violated by segregated schools. *Brown vs. the Board of Education's* greatest gift, then, was not desegregation itself, but the societal understanding that came about as a result of the decision.

This process of changing social thought through law, in my mind, has many possibilities for the future of civil rights. For example, I would like to push for a federal hate crimes law, which might instill an absolute and distinct abhorrence of crimes based on race, gender, or sexuality. I also hope to help initiate legislation that would allow gays and lesbians to marry; decades after that happens, people may wonder why anyone ever opposed such laws. I truly believe that the path to universal civil rights begins in the law, the basis of those rights.

As a socially conscious person, I must choose between changing a moment and changing the world. Individual protests may cause a few individuals or a community to think about a given issue for a few more minutes than usual, but legal change subtly influences the *way* in which this society thinks. Perceptions and morals, over time, are shaped by the way this country legislates civil rights. This theory can work in a negative way; the sodomy laws that still exist in a few states help people to rationalize homophobia. I believe, however, that societal values translated from law can function in a positive fashion, and it is this phenomenon that I hope to use in my work as an attorney.

Northwestern University School of Law

M. Angela Buenaventura

Angela transferred from Grinnell College to Oglethorpe University during her junior year. She majored in economics and was a member of the Beta Omicron Sigma Business Honorary Society. She served as both format manager for her college's radio station and copy editor for the college music publication. Angela was also a member of Amnesty International. She planned to work at a nonprofit organization for a year before attending Northwestern University.

Stats:

LSAT: 165

GPA: 3.83 (economics)

College attended: Oglethorpe University

Class: 2002

Hometown: Atlanta, GA

Gender: Female

Race: Hispanic

Law school attending: Northwestern University School of Law

Class: 2006

Applied to the following law schools:

Accepted: Boston College, Emory, Georgetown, Northwestern, University of Georgia, University of Michigan

Denied: None

Other: None

Personal statement:

According to Angela, the prompts for which she wrote her personal statement all "were something to this effect: 'Please present yourself, your background and experiences, and your ideas as you wish in a brief personal statement.'"

I was sitting on my bed studying for a chemistry test one night when my sister knocked on my bedroom door. She said that she and my parents needed to talk to me about something. A chill went down my spine, and I thought someone must have died. I would have never guessed that I'd be having the conversation that followed.

As it turns out, my family immigrated here illegally. I have lived in the United States since I was two years old and had never questioned my citizenship status, but my parents informed me that immigration restrictions would soon be tightened and that I should undergo immigrations proceedings before these stricter laws came into place. The next day, I skipped my chemistry test and went to the Immigration and Naturalization Service office downtown to turn myself in as an undocumented alien. I was fingerprinted, interviewed, and photographed. When I left INS building that day, I was scared out my sixteen-year-old mind.

Over the next several months, I spent endless hours in overcrowded INS waiting rooms. I also spent countless hours on the Internet, reading about immigration history and law and trying to interpret what would happen to my sister and me. During my senior year of high school, I was awarded conditional residency. My lawyer told me that I would eventually be awarded permanent residency, but there was no telling when. Finally, during my freshman year of college, I was awarded permanent resident status.

Somewhere in this dizzying stream of events, something clicked. I wanted to learn more about the laws that shaped my life as an immigrant. I signed up for an immigration history class during my sophomore year of college, and although my favorite classes had previously been math-and-science based, this immigration history class fascinated me. The next semester, I designed an independent study project that focused on modern immigration law from 1965 to the present. I have always enjoyed the sciences because they allow me to better understand everyday phenomena, and immigration history provides yet another lens through which to see the world around me. A quotation printed at the top of my immigration history syllabus still sticks with me today. "Once I thought to write a history of the immigrants in America. Then I discovered that the immigrants were American history" (Oscar Handlin, Introduction to *The Uprooted*, 1951). I want to study law for intellectual satisfaction. I want to practice law to help provide others with the opportunities I have enjoyed in the U.S.

Sandra

Sandra graduated summa cum laude from Cornell University with a degree in English literature. She won several essay prizes for her work on British drama, including recognition for the best senior thesis in English, and was involved in the performance of both choral and instrumental music. Her experience volunteering as a conversation partner for Cornell's ESL program led her to South Korea, where she spent a year teaching conversational English through the Fulbright program.

Stats:
LSAT: 166, 171
GPA: 3.86
College attended: Cornell University
Class: 2001
Hometown: Philadelphia, PA
Gender: Female
Race: White
Law school attending: Northwestern University School of Law
Class: 2005

Applied to the following law schools:
Accepted: Harvard, Northwestern, Stanford, University of South Carolina, University of Virginia
Denied: None
Other: University of Chicago, University of Michigan (placed on waitlist by both)

Personal statement:
According to Sandra, "I used my statement for all the law schools I applied to; I recall that all of them had the general 'tell us about yourself' personal statement instead of a specific question."

"Korea? Why are you in Korea?" my friend's voice echoed down the line. I was a month into my year as a Fulbright English Teaching Assistant, and though I readily recited the answer on my grant application—the desire to gain perspective on my own culture and education by experiencing the "other side" of a classroom—my friend remained unconvinced. "You want to be a lawyer," she continued. "What's teaching in Korea got to do with that?" Her challenge silenced me; I had no easy answer for that question at the time. However, I now realize that although my legal career might end up having nothing to do with Korea, teaching here has affirmed my ambition to be a lawyer by transforming my views of the uses of language and consequently of the law.

My passion for language, and thus for literature, has long been a shaping force in my life. As a child, I constantly had bruised knees—the result of maximizing my book time by reading while walking. My bookish ways continued throughout middle and high school, and I was stereotyped as "the reader," "the writer," and naturally, "the English major." I rebelled against these assumptions in my first years of college, sampling anthropology, cognitive psychology, and computer science as potential majors. Yet my rebellion was a failure; I realize now that even these seemingly diverse fields are also abstract ways of thinking about language. However, I prefer the particular, and eventually I ended up majoring in English literature as predicted. My studies sharpened and deepened my liking for words as I tracked shifting narrative tone, searched for puns, and burrowed through layers of meaning, and I became interested in law because I saw it as an opportunity to continue working with words and using the intellectual skills I learned as an English major.

Consequently, when I came to Korea I fondly viewed language as an aesthetic object, and thought the enjoyment of my job would come from coaxing the same view out of my students. But as I quickly learned in my classroom, English can be a slippery and treacherous thing. My students have only studied the language for two years, and to them, English seems like a massive maze deliberately constructed to frustrate them. Why, they ask, can "must" only be used in the present tense? Why are "bread" and "chalk" uncountable nouns? Too often, I can only answer "Because," and my view of language becomes a little bit more like that of my students' each time. On my best days as a teacher, I feel that I have guided my students successfully through the maze, and that English is a tool that I am helping my students to use rather than an object for my intellectual contemplation. As an English major, I ferreted out the complexities of language, but now I seek its simplicities.

In the same way, my view of law has shifted. My intellectual curiosity and pleasure in words still draw me to the subject, but the lawyer's roles as guide and protector also attract me now. Before I began teaching, I rarely gave credit to practical applications, but I now see language and law as tools to be used as well as studied.

Similarly, teaching has shown me that using my understanding to assist other people increases that comprehension in ways I could not have anticipated. My friend's questions may once have puzzled me, but I now know that even though I came to Korea without thought to my future career, my time teaching here has given me a direction and purpose in the law.

Darren Spedale

Darren is a magna cum laude graduate of Duke University with extensive work experience, including service with a law firm and the U.S. Senate. He also attended the University of Copenhagen on a Fulbright Fellowship, where he wrote a book on Denmark as the first country to legalize same-sex marriage.

Stats:

LSAT: 167

GPA: 3.65

College attended: Duke University

Class: Did not report

Hometown: New York, NY

Gender: Male

Race: White

Law school attending: Stanford Law School (J.D./M.B.A.)

Class: 2004

Applied to the following law schools:

Accepted: Columbia, Duke, Georgetown, NYU, Stanford

Denied: None

Other: None

Personal statement:

According to Darren, the prompt for his personal statement was "open-ended."

"If there was one thing I would have like to have been able to keep," said Jens, slowly and thoughtfully, "it would have been his silk pajamas." He turned away from me to look down at the floor, with a slight gleam in his eye and the faintest of smiles on his lips. "I can't tell you how many times I fell asleep feeling that silk against the side of my face," he sighed.

During our 3-hour interview, I learned a great deal about Jens' life with Niels. I learned of how they had met working as attendants in Tivoli, Copenhagen's 500-year old amusement park. I learned many amusing stories about the 12 wonderful years they shared together as a couple. And I learned of the horror that Jens faced when, on May 13, 1984, Niels finally succumbed to AIDS after a two-year struggle.

Yet for Jens, the real horror was not in the countless hours, weeks and months of having to feed Niels and clean up after him, only to watch him waste away. "That much, at least, I had prepared myself for, as best I could," Jens told me. The true nightmare began after his death, when a document appeared under his door from a lawyer representing Niels' parents.

As Jens explained, Niels' parents had never accepted that their son was gay. They had broken off contact with Niels soon after he moved in with Jens, and told him that they didn't want to see him until he was no longer living with another man. Since then, they had spoken together only once a year, when Niels called every December to wish them a merry Christmas.

The letter, it turns out, was a demand by the parents for Jens to relinquish all of Niels' belongings. "They couldn't stand the idea that their son's personal items were all with me," said Jens. "They wanted to take it from me, just because they couldn't accept their son for the way he was. They wanted to take from me all I had left of him, after all those years of living together."

Although he enlisted the help of a lawyer friend to fight off the parents' demand, a judge ruled that, as there was no legislation recognizing same-sex couples and there was no will, the parents had the right to take back their son's belongings. "And so all I could do was stand there and watch as the movers took it all," said Jens, his voice cracking. "The furniture we shared, the books he loved, and even those silk pajamas I knew so well. If it had only been five years later, none of this would ever have happened!"

This is why I had come to Denmark – to learn of the injustices suffered by same-sex couples over the past several decades, and to find out how the landmark 1989 Law on Registered Partnership changed history, both in Scandinavia and abroad.

Recognizing the disparity in Danish family law, the Danish parliament a decade ago passed the partnership law, which was the first of its kind in the world. It grants same-sex couples all the rights and responsibilities of marriage if they register their relationship with the state. Thus, by walking down the aisle in any city hall in Denmark and exchanging vows in front of a government official and two witnesses, a same-sex couple can now be covered by the same legal protections their heterosexual counterparts enjoy.

I first learned of this progressive piece of legislation as an undergraduate, while finishing my Senior Honors Thesis on domestic partnership benefits available in the United States. (At the time, in the mid '90s, less than 20 major public and private organizations offered such benefits. Now, almost a decade later, the number of employers offering such benefits numbers in the hundreds.) After doing some research on the Danish legislation, I began to sense that the Law on Registered Partnership was to become a blueprint model for other countries interested in passing comprehensive legislation for same-sex couples.

After graduation, while spending a year as a legal assistant at the branch of Milbank Tweed in Washington DC, I sometimes found myself staying after-hours to use the law library's resources in an attempt to learn more about the Danish legislation. However, while I was able to locate a few documents detailing the *contents* of the legislation, I soon found that nobody had conducted research in regards to the *results* of the legislation. Considering the growing interest in the USA and other countries in same-sex marriage, I felt that knowing how the world's first 'gay marriage' law functioned in practice would be a piece of information crucial to those in other countries considering similar legislation.

Thus, with the assistance of a Fulbright Fellowship and admission to the law school of the University of Copenhagen, I set out to find out what could be learned from the first country in the world to grant same-sex couples the rights and responsibilities of marriage. To my surprise, no research attempts had as yet been made to look into this question; my research, then, was to be mainly of an empirical nature.

Having become fluent in Danish in preparation for this venture, I spent the first several months of my stay huddled over a desk in a number of basement newspaper and journal archives, acquiring additional background knowledge that had been unavailable to me in the USA. This consisted of gathering as much information as I could on the history of the partnership law, from its earliest conception in the 1960's to its passage in 1989. In addition, my earliest courses at the law school focused on introducing me to the workings of Nordic and European law, concepts that would be important to my perspective on the Danish partnership law.

The bulk of my research, however, was to consist of interviews, to determine how the partnership law had become integrated into everyday life in Denmark, and to what extent there had been problems during the years of the law's implementation. This involved interviews with dozens of people in some way connected to the law – from members of parliament to bureaucrats at the Ministry of Justice, from newspaper journalists to Christian fundamentalists, and from lobbyists in the country's gay and lesbian organization to those who have entered into partnerships themselves.

It was the stories told by this last group – couples who have actually 'tied the knot' – which I found the most compelling. The richness and diversity of tales told by people in the 20 couples I interviewed around the country could form a book in themselves. And while I had always found the Danish law impressive, even before coming to the country, it was only through the individual connections I made with the people who had been personally touched by the law that I came to understand how important this law has been for so many people in terms of giving them the control to live their lives as they wished, with the contentment that their families – some with children, others without – were legally secure.

The powerful stories conveyed to me by these couples, combined with the surprising volume of new information I uncovered about same-sex marriage in Denmark, convinced me to change the goal of my Fulbright experience from writing a paper for a legal journal to writing a book for publication. The extensive amount of significant information to be drawn from the Danish experience with same-sex marriage, I decided, warranted more space than I could give it in a paper.

My experience with the Danish legislation only worked to increase my interest in this type of progressive legislation. Upon my return to the states I was employed by the office of Senator Paul Wellstone in Washington DC, where among other things I worked on seeking out Senate co-sponsors for his domestic partnership bill. The bill, which would extend limited spousal benefits such as health care coverage to the domestic partners of federal employees, was a far cry from the type of legislation I had just spent two years researching. Yet considering the extremely small number of Senators I found willing to sponsor even such limited legislation as the Wellstone bill, it seems that a great deal of work still needs to be done before same-sex couples here in the USA will enjoy the legal possibilities available to their counterparts in Northern Europe.

Nevertheless, I feel that I have been truly blessed to have been given the opportunity to research and write about a topic as timely and as fascinating as same-sex marriage. The development of 'non-traditional family law' (as I tend to call it) over the past couple of decades holds a great deal of interest to me, and I can easily see myself becoming an advocate for those whom the field of family law has traditionally overlooked – not only same-sex couples, but single parents, unmarried cohabitants, and others who face uncertainty in the absence of protective legislation.

Jens, unfortunately, passed away from complications due to AIDS in 1998, a year after our interview together. Yet thanks to the existence of the Danish partnership law, all of his belongings passed on to Jakob, his partner since 1988, whom he had 'married' in 1991. It is to the memory of Jens, and to all those that have helped enact and taken advantage of the Danish legislation, that I dedicate my research. And I remain hopeful that, in the not-too-distant future, we can work to secure similar possibilities here in the United States, and to ensure that such tragedies as those experienced by Jens in 1984 are relegated to the history books.

Svetla Petkova

Svetla, a native of Bulgaria, pursued legal studies with high distinction in France. She transferred to the United States to join her family in 1995. Svetla received numerous academic awards while in college. For three years she worked as a legal assistant/global relocation specialist at Dechert Law Firm.

Stats:

LSAT: 156

GPA: 4.0 (area studies)

College attended: Drexel University

Hometown: Bulgaria

Gender: Female

Race: White

Law school attending: The George Washington University Law School

Class: 2005

Applied to the following law schools:

Accepted: George Washington University

Denied: None

Other: None

Personal statement:

(From The George Washington University Law School application for admission)

"All applicants are required to submit a personal statement, which should include any additional information you think might be of assistance to the Admissions Committee in considering your application. Examples of such information are significant extracurricular or community activities, the reasons why you want to study law, a discussion of your background, or an explanation of any unusual aspects of your academic record. This statement must be written on separate pages and must accompany this application."

"I will never give up my convictions." These were the last words of my great-grandfather, Ilia Stefanov, judge and candidate for the Bulgarian Parliament, before he was assassinated by the Communists in 1945. Heir of a long tradition of West

European-educated lawyers and advocate for the plurality of political structures, he had refused to collaborate with the dictatorial regime. In the following 45 years under totalitarianism, members of my family were banned from practicing law. The story of this proud man, whose eyes looked at me inquisitively from an old black and white picture, fired my imagination into a burning desire to return to the tradition of legal practice in my family. What started as a romantic idea of youth became the beginning of a quest for knowledge and personal growth.

I grew up in Bulgaria in the last decades of the Iron Curtain, in a dictatorial system that did not allow ideas and opinions to diverge from the communist dogma. Early on I learned the meaning of the concept "forbidden": music, books, movies from the "West" or with dissident ideas, names of scientists and writers, as well as facts of world history and scientific discoveries, were forbidden. The hardest part for me was growing up with the fear that I belonged to a different family, a family that had lost several members killed or sent to camps by the communists. As a result, being a third generation of that family, many venues in life were closed forever for me. In retrospect, I feel blessed to have parents who showed me at that time the truth behind the mask of the regime.

I was attending the French High School in Sofia in 1989, when the winds of change brought events that turned the world I knew upside down. As Eastern Europe embraced dramatic political changes, I welcomed my first free vote with exultation. The passionate speeches I gave at political debates in school and the reading of then incomprehensible political documents were remarkable lessons in civic duties and political consciousness.

Following the debates surrounding the drafting of a new constitution, I learned that law was not just an abstract text, but a process that embodies various interests. I researched definitions of civil rights and mechanisms to protect them, realizing the limitations of a constitution that reflected the social tides of a particular era. As I witnessed the struggle of an entire nation to establish the democratic structures of its new society, my desire for a career in law grew steadily. In 1992, I was accepted with honors at the University of Sofia, having won the prestigious National Competition in Literature, and I successfully participated in my country's first competitive exams for admission to French universities. At that time my dream to study law within a long-established judicial system was stronger than ever, and I chose to pursue my studies in France.

When the train pulled into the station at Nancy, France, I knew I had started an extraordinary journey. During my three years studying law at the University of Nancy, I absorbed the fascinating history of the French legal system, the logic and precision of law and the influence of social perceptions and historical circumstances on legal principles. I continued to research and relate French laws to those developing in Bulgaria, thus broadening my interest in the comparison of legal systems and the search for unifying principles.

My experience in France was a rite of passage from adolescence to adulthood. Coming from a small and rather homogeneous nation, I discovered the meaning of being "the other" and being "different." To break cultural barriers, I hastened to learn about West European history, politics, economics and society. This motivation reflected also in my role as a co-founder of the first organization for business and cultural relations between Nancy and Bulgaria. In the process I rediscovered a sense of me that was stronger than I have ever known. Thrown into a new culture and away from my family, self-reliance became a way of being. I worked at night to support myself and was twice as proud to achieve honors in an educational system where only one-third of the students were promoted to a higher level each year and where I was the only student for whom French was not a native tongue. Eager to apply my knowledge, I persuaded an international company to utilize my legal skills and was thus introduced to the practical legal world. There I focused on the interpretation and use of legal principles in the functioning of a business unit of society - the corporation.

In 1995, while I was visiting my parents who were working in the United States at that time, the former communist party regained power in Bulgaria. I had to make a quick and radical decision about my life. "My country is the one where I feel Freedom," Benjamin Franklin had said. For me this country became America. I was fascinated that people from different races, religions and cultures live and work side by side. I realized that I was not "the other" here. Once again, I challenged myself to learn a new language on my own, and to adapt rapidly to a new educational, social and cultural system. At last, I could satisfy my longing for knowledge in areas, such as psychology, philosophy, anthropology, and foreign politics, which were banned by the communists. I wanted to understand the human psyche, the social forces and political circumstances to be an effective legal practitioner. Thus, I enrolled in the International Area Studies program at Drexel University to study the historical, political and cultural fabric of American society, and to relate it to foreign politics, economics, and cultures. My studies in this rigorous program, which focused on research and writing, alternated with full-time cooperative work as a Paralegal, and I soon excelled in both.

After graduating *summa cum laude*, I immediately landed a position as Legal Assistant at Dechert Immigration Group, one of the leading immigration law practices in the U.S. Mastering the vocabulary and intricacies of immigration law was a challenging task that has provided me with a unique perspective on the application of law to the individual. I have researched legal precedents, analyzed complex case issues, communicated opinions and written persuasive documents to advocate the merit of outstanding researchers, investors, and people with exceptional abilities who further the United States' economic, medical, scientific, and artistic progress. Recognizing the value of my creative and independent work, the attorneys have promoted me to the position of Global Relocation Specialist. Responsible for more than two hundred corporate and individual clients, I have learned the discipline, precision and minute attention to detail that are critical for the study of law.

In making my choices in life, I have constantly sought challenge and growth. I have overcome economic, cultural and social obstacles while proving to myself that there are no heights that cannot be reached. Through my academic training and "real life" experiences, I have learned firsthand how law applies to all layers of the social structure. Today, my thirst for knowledge in the sphere of international legal affairs is ever growing. This is an area where my diverse background and abilities will find the best realization. Combining an U.S. law degree with my European law expertise will enable me in many ways to contribute to a better global understanding and cooperation. I am convinced that the universality of many legal principles creates bridges between nations. I would like to walk such bridges with a deeper sense of fulfillment, having given all my efforts to promote the freedom of creativity and to eliminate the borders of prejudice and discrimination. I want to look at that picture of my great-grandfather with pride, knowing that I too will practice the noble profession of law, in freedom, in the country, which is my home.

Jennifer A. Pursley

Jennifer was active in theater and dance at Eastern Arizona College, where she completed her first two years of college. After taking a year off to stay home with her first child, she attended the University of Alaska—Anchorage for one year. She then took another two years off to spend more time with her growing family and worked part time for the preservation department of the Marriott Library in Salt Lake City, Utah. She took another year and a half to finish her B.A. in English at the University of Utah. After a six-week stint in the Air Force, she worked for a year as the office manager for a small construction and design firm in Tucson, Arizona, the hometown of the law school in which she completed her law degree.

Stats:

LSAT: 161

GPA: 3.09

Colleges attended: Eastern Arizona College, University of Alaska—Anchorage, University of Utah

Class: 1998

Hometown: Tuscon, AZ

Gender: Female

Race: White

Law school attending: University of Arizona—James E. Rogers College of Law

Class: 2002

Applied to the following law schools:

Accepted: Lewis and Clark Northwestern School of Law, Thomas M. Cooley Law School, University of Arizona

Denied: None

Other: None

Personal statement:

Jennifer did not write her personal statement in response to any particular question.

My parents were working to instill in me an awareness and appreciation of the rich cultural diversity that exists in the Western US long before I was aware of the concept of diversity. My father earned his teaching degree when he was thirty and I was five; in August of that year, we set off on the first of what my parents liked to call our "adventures". My dad got his first teaching job in Chinle, Arizona, on the Navajo Reservation. The first thing I remember seeing as we drove into town is an old Navajo couple in traditional dress driving along the side of the road in a beat-up wooden wagon pulled by two horses; having spent the first part of my life in Phoenix and Salt Lake City, this was an amazing sight to me.

The next thing that stands out in my mind is my first day in Navajo Culture class when all the students got to find out what clan they belonged to. All the little Navajo children were from clans with the names of fierce or cunning animals like bear or fox, but I, the Anglo, the biligana, was from the White clan whose symbol is a sack of grain. Imagine my disappointment, to find out that while all the other kids had clans that were known for their bravery, strength, or intelligence, and had symbols that were at least animate, I belonged to a clan that was known for wanting to eat and was symbolized by a feedbag. This was the first time that I really became aware that each culture has its own set of values and judges other cultures by those values.

My appreciation for people's differing ideals was reinforced as my parents' adventures took me to the Apache Reservation, an Inupiat Eskimo village, border towns in two states, several rural areas in Arizona, an Alaskan homesteading settlement, and a Upik Eskimo village. I was taught to say, "Hello, friend" and "I love you" in five different languages. I cooked blue corn soup, wove miniature rugs, sewed mukluks out of moose hide and beaver fur, rode in dog sleds down huge frozen rivers, broke piñatas to celebrate Posada, sang songs for a good harvest, did square dances, and tied quilts.

My parents' adventures added many interesting experiences to my childhood, but they also helped me to develop my own personal values. Having frequently been the only member of my race in a classroom, or the only person unable to speak the popular language, I value tolerance very highly. I also place a high value on respect for individuals, as well as for their cultures; I have learned that every culture and every group is made up of individuals who deserve to be treated as individuals, and not judged by the popular conception or historic depiction of their group or culture. I have discovered that, by surrounding myself with people from various places, cultures, educational and professional backgrounds, and generations, I learn more about the world, humanity, and myself.

My parents also taught me the value of determination, persistence, and hard work. They both went to college, worked as many hours as they could and built a family with five children, all at the same time. It took them both more than a decade, but they earned their baccalaureates. Then they each went on for their Masters', and they still take classes whenever time and place permit. Their example was an important lesson on the value of education.

I have many interests, and during my middle school and high school years, I took advantage of every opportunity I could to study new subjects. I took a broad range of classes, joined a variety of clubs and activities, and competed in several competitions. My favorite subject was French, and I placed nationally both years I competed in *Le Grand Concours* French Competition. When I started college, my major was Foreign Language, but I continued to pursue my various interests through courses and activities. I was one of the founders of the French Club at Eastern Arizona College, as well as its president. I was a member of the repertory theater company and the Renaissance dance troupe with whom I performed at the Arizona Renaissance Festival. I tutored for both French and English. I had a wonderful time and did well in my classes. I got to know my professors and the other students. I was enjoying learning in many different areas of my life.

After the responsibilities of marriage and family forced me to slow down for a few years, it was with tremendous relief, joy, and quite a bit of pride, that I received my diploma last winter. I worked hard for my education, and it was worth the work. I intend to keep working hard for my professional degree and for my continuing education because education has great value to me, and because I want it to have value to my children.

I have chosen to pursue legal education because it offers the opportunity to become a member of an honored and intellectually intriguing profession in which I can use my talents and the skills I acquired in my undergraduate studies. The college courses I found most interesting and rewarding were those that emphasized writing textual analyses using a theoretical framework with research for supporting evidence. Through my experience with different groups of people, I have learned to look at issues from multiple perspectives. One of the things I find fascinating in building written arguments is that there is rarely any true right or wrong answer; an answer is only as right as the writer can convincingly prove it is. I love exploring the possible arguments made available by viewing textual evidence from different perspectives.

I believe that the study of law involves a similar process, and I would enjoy improving my skills while learning the practical application that legal study provides. I look forward to studying with other students who share my ideals of fairness, honesty, hard work, and integrity. I hope to be an active and influential member of workgroups where teamwork, dedication, tenacity, and an open mind are common traits. The same strength of character, intelligence, sense of humor, and resiliency that has helped me reach my past goals, both academically and person-ally, will help me attain my future goals and become an asset to my community and to the legal profession.

Paul Samoni

Paul made the Dean's List seven straight semesters and is a member of five honor societies, including Phi Beta Kappa. During his senior year, he researched, wrote, edited, and published an independent historical analysis titled Pennsylvania Mennonites in Frontier Virginia: Migrations, Settlements, and "Success" (1699–1825). *After graduating magna cum laude, he spent four years working for Wells Fargo Bank and one year working as a contractor for Capital International's Private Equity program.*

Stats:
LSAT: 157
GPA: 3.75 (history)
College attended: Rutgers University—Rutgers College
Class: 1995
Hometown: Mt. Laurel, NJ
Gender: Male
Race: White
Law school attending: University of California—Davis School of Law
Class: 2005

Applied to the following law schools:
Accepted: Loyola Law School, Rutgers, Southwestern University, University of California—Davis
Denied: University of California—Hastings, University of Georgia
Other: None

Personal statement:
Paul did not report writing his personal statement in response to any particular question.

In September 1996, I decided to visit my older brother in San Francisco, California. Days before I boarded the airplane to visit the West Coast for the first time, I convinced myself that this was nothing more than a vacation. As a recent college graduate who had just left a dead-end job, I viewed this excursion merely as respite from making a decision about what I was going to do with the rest of my life. Little did I know it was an opportunity to take the next step in my life's journey.

I was born and raised on the East Coast, the seventh of eight children. In 1983, our family moved from Western Pennsylvania to Mount Laurel, New Jersey. For the next thirteen years of my life, I lived within two hours of New York City, and thirty minutes of Philadelphia. I attended Rutgers College, which is a school that attracts students from all types of backgrounds. Obviously, I was always surrounded by diversity. Unfortunately, I rarely took the initiative to embrace it.

Throughout high school and college, I was often too involved with my studies and my own friends to see what else the world had to offer. This is not to say that attending Rutgers was a mistake. I made many new and lasting friendships, and I think I took full advantage of the wonderful faculty and extensive academic resources a large school like Rutgers has to offer. I took my lumps during my first year, but as soon as I adjusted to my surroundings, I consistently achieved significant academic success. In retrospect, when I graduated in the spring of 1995, I understood what it takes to succeed in college. I had not missed many opportunities to excel in the classroom, but as I would discover later, there is more to learning than just midterms and essays. And I had a lot to learn.

Shortly after graduation, I returned to the safe haven of Mount Laurel to plan my next move. I considered graduate school and went to a few job interviews, but I was not getting closer to determining my next step. My older brother in San Francisco sensed I was becoming complacent, so he invited me to visit him and explore California. "Bob (his partner) and I aren't getting any younger, and neither are you," he warned.

My brother and his partner welcomed me at the airport, and drove me to their house. Sitting on the desk in my room was a copy of my resume. Apparently, they expected me to stay a bit longer than I had planned. We went to dinner, and my brother lectured me on the fine art of the interview. We spent the rest of the weekend sightseeing, but my brother knocked on my door at 6 a.m. Monday morning. I spent the rest of my "vacation" sending out resumes and preparing for interviews.

It took some time, but my brother's faith in me and his motivation convinced me to persevere. I soon became determined to find a job and stake my claim in

California. My first break came in October, when I was hired as a temporary employee in the Retail Division of Wells Fargo Bank. I soon worked my way up to a full-time position. To say the least, it was thrilling to land a real job. My first position with the Bank allowed me an opportunity to interact with team members from all over the country, from branch tellers in San Diego to vice presidents in Phoenix. When I moved to the systems side in 1999, I had an opportunity to broaden my knowledge and to gain exposure to the fast-paced world of high-tech. In short, working at Wells Fargo was a valuable experience because it marked the beginning of my professional growth. However, more importantly, my brother's trust in me proved to be contagious. No matter what the future holds for me, I now know that I can succeed in an academic, a professional, and even a technical environment. Before I arrived in the Bay Area, I had not realized this.

Of course, my first years in San Francisco were not merely all work and no play. The three of us participated in numerous activities, including bowling. A few weeks after I informed them of my decision to stay, Bob and Joe drafted me into a gay bowling league. At first, my reaction to this announcement was one of annoyance. Although I am a HUGE sports fan, I did not ask my brother and his partner to enroll me in a gay bowling league. I was new to the Bay Area, and I could think of a plethora of other things I'd rather do with my "spare" time. Furthermore, I had bowled no more than a handful of times, so I doubted my participation would assist their team. Besides, why would a straight (and slightly stuffy, I must confess) guy want to hang out with a bunch of homosexual bowlers? "It will be fun," they assured me. I doubted that.

We played every Wednesday at the old Japantown Bowl in San Francisco. Our team ("The Pin Pals") consisted of two other players and our family: my brother, his partner, and me. We finished the season in last place with an atrocious record, and my average peaked at 117. Indeed, this was a pathetic display of bowling skills. Nonetheless, it was a blast. I could have stayed home every Wednesday and watched reruns on Nick at Nite. Instead, I got a chance to get out and meet someone new every week. This may not appear to be a major accomplishment, but it was something I rarely did, even in college. Many of our opponents enjoyed spectator sports almost as much as I did. Some of them were young and just starting out on their own. A few grew up on the East Coast and appreciated how difficult it is to find a decent cheesesteak place in California. I soon learned the people in the league were no different from my other friends or me. They just happened to be better bowlers.

I have formed numerous lasting friendships since my arrival in the Bay Area, but none is more special than the one I have developed with my fiancée Dalisay. An immigrant from the Philippines, she is a spunky, enthusiastic 5-foot tall dynamo. She came to this country alone to pursue a career in nursing and spent her first year working at a nursing home in Texas. She shared an apartment with seven other nurses and slept in a bed that was in the closet. I met her shortly after she moved to California when she was in the process of leaving a nursing home position to start her first job as a full-time staff nurse in a hospital. When she told me about her life in America so far, I was amazed at how well she had adjusted in such a short time. I was also unaware that she was just getting started. In the past three years, she returned to school full-time and accepted a nursing position in the prestigious University of California San Francisco Health System. In May, she received her Master's degree and became a Certified Nurse Practitioner. Her hard work and positive attitude have proved to be an inspiration to me. I have considered post-graduate education for quite some time, but I guess I just needed someone to remind and encourage me to follow my dreams. Thanks to Dalisay, I am in the process of doing that.

As noted on my resume, I left Wells Fargo in late October 2000. My position with Wells Fargo required me to perform overtime and my responsibilities were numerous and demanding. I did not think I would be able to remain fully dedicated to my job and my coworkers while preparing for my future aspirations, so I tendered my resignation. During the past eleven months, I have been fortunate to find a temporary niche as a contract employee at The Capital Group in San Francisco. During my brief assignment, I have been exposed to the worlds of Private Equity and Mutual Funds, and I have gained a better understanding of finance, stock markets, economics and the like. In addition, I've been able to see how diverse a career in law can be (my current manager, a Vice President and Investor Relations Manager in the Private Equity Group, spent over 16 years as a lawyer and investment banker). I plan to remain with Capital until the Fall semester, and I am pleased to work in an environment where I am able to continue to learn something new every day (for example, I recently found out that soju, a distilled liquor made from steamed rice, is Korea's top-selling alcoholic beverage).

Since my graduation in the spring of 1995, I have had many adventures and accomplished a lot in such a short time. My future is a bright one, and I consider myself fortunate to have numerous career options from which to choose. So why am

I interested in pursuing a law degree rather than something else? I could fill more than five double-spaced, typewritten pages answering that question, but I realize you are a busy person. In short, a law career would allow me to use the professional skills I have developed so far and provide an opportunity to make a difference in all kinds of ways. Furthermore, I am intrigued by the almost limitless possibilities of a law career. Although I am unsure of what field of law I would like to practice, my decision to apply is not based on a desire to escape my current situation. If anything, I hope this essay proves that I succeeded inside and outside the office. By attending law school, I want to build on that success, continue learning and try something new again. I realize that law school can be as demanding as any full-time job, and that is why I wanted to take a step back and ensure that this is something I truly am prepared to do. I have had significant time to explore the United States, visit family and friends, prepare for a June wedding and ponder my future. I am confident that Law School is the next step for me, and I welcome the new challenges and experiences it can provide.

What an eventful five years! I formed new friendships, announced my engagement, developed professional and social skills and I have become closer to my brother and his partner. Throughout it all, I think I have grown as a person. After all, before I boarded that airplane in 1996, I pondered my future with uncertainty and trepidation. Today, as I sit here adding the finishing touches to this essay, I am eager to see what happens next.

Mark Allan Pickering

Mark graduated with honors from and received the Edwin Smith Hinkley Scholarship at Brigham Young University. He worked for three semesters as a teaching or research assistant for his professors. He interrupted college for two years to serve in Frankfurt, Germany, as a missionary for the Church of Jesus Christ of Latter-day Saints.

Stats:

LSAT: 168
GPA: 3.91 (political science)
College attended: Brigham Young University
Class: 2002
Hometown: Arlington, TX
Gender: Male
Race: White
Law school attending: University of Chicago Law School
Class: 2005

Applied to the following law schools:

Accepted: Columbia, NYU, University of Chicago, University of Texas
Denied: Yale

Other: Stanford, University of Michigan, University of Virginia (placed on waitlist by all). Harvard offered Mark a place on the waitlist, but he declined.

Personal statement:

Mark did not report writing his personal statement in response to any particular question.

There was a time in eighth grade, shortly after the riots in Los Angeles that followed the acquittal of police officers accused of brutality in beating Rodney King, when the school administration decided they needed to call an assembly in order to explain things. I sat obediently through the proceedings and agreed with the condemnation of rioting: "Rioting is just stupid," said one student. But when the police officer speaking to us and responding to student comments off-handedly dismissed the court proceedings that acquitted the officers as obviously flawed, I decided I had to say something. I raised my hand, was called on, and then stood up. In a somewhat feeble voice (there were a lot of people in there), I said, "None of us was at the trial or saw the evidence. I think we ought to trust the courts and not condemn what we haven't seen." Silence and rude glares followed, but no responses came.

My professors, fellow-parishioners, and classmates – if they know me at all – know me as one who thinks for himself. In my tenth grade American literature class we were discussing John Steinbeck's *Grapes of Wrath*. When asked to present commentary on a section that compared Jefferson and Madison with Lenin and Marx, I registered my disagreement. The members of my class were somewhat irritated – you weren't supposed to *disagree* with the author!

Now, I wasn't disagreeing to be disagreeable – I really believed what I was saying. I was disturbed people were willing to believe the book because it was in print. But most importantly of all, it did not bother me that I disagreed. I remained convinced of my view because no one satisfactorily refuted my arguments.

Teachers didn't always like me in High School. I guess I disputed too much. Teachers in college love me – they seem to think no one here disputes enough. Here is an atypical example: a few weeks ago a professor of mine felt obligated to apologize for the Supreme Court's use of the word "imbeciles" to describe mentally disabled people. I told him it was a technical term that specified mental ability according to IQ. He didn't believe me, so I looked it up. He looked it up as well. An imbecile is a person with a mental age of eight to twelve.

Often I find myself to be the only one in a classroom willing to defend an unpopular point of view. Once a visiting lecturer in one of my small classes criticized libertarianism. I found myself sticking up for it. At BYU, I find myself in certain situations to be the only one who is willing to speak for theistic evolution.

I suppose this propensity to think for myself has always existed, but I think my experience in Germany strengthened it. When in Germany, I had the opportunity to speak with an American accountant whom a large German company had hired. He described his difficulty in getting his coworkers to switch to Generally Accepted Accounting Practices (GAAP). I then rejoined, "Then just imagine how difficult it is to get them to believe in the Book of Mormon!" He merely shook his head, stupefied. "I can imagine…" he said.

Sometimes my companion in the mission field and I were the only Latter-day Saints for miles. For hours, days, and weeks on end, we would be unable to find any one interested in listening to us. Occasionally came a shrill rebuke, especially from elderly men, "Why don't you go find something worthwhile to do? You're just wasting your time!" At first it was quite discouraging, but after several months I found myself quite accustomed to acting as only I found appropriate. People ignored me as I tried to stop them in pedestrian zones. It became a challenge to get past barriers people erected to keep out solicitations from strangers.

I found when I returned after two years that this experience had permanently changed the way I dealt with resistance to or criticism of my views. I respond with emotional indifference now. This combined with my previous and current indepen-dence of mind has been a gift that has allowed me to think and pursue what I think is right no matter what the opposition.

Stephanie Ladd

Stephanie worked the overnight shift full time at a software company during her undergraduate years to pay her way through school; she also had two years of bookkeeping/ accounting experience. In her last year of college, she received a prestigious travel fellowship for archaeological research in Italy. She also pointed out in her application that she was a first-generation college graduate.

Stats:

LSAT: 161

College GPA: 3.5 (classics)

College attended: University of Colorado—Boulder

Class: 2001

Hometown: Santa Fe, NM

Gender: Female

Race: White

Law school attending: University of Colorado—Boulder School of Law

Class: 2005

Applied to the following law schools:

Accepted: Lewis and Clark College (Northwestern School of Law), University of Colorado—Boulder, University of Miami, Washington University in St. Louis

Denied: None

Other: None

Personal statement:

In Stephanie's words, "I used the same essay for each school; the topic for the CU—Boulder essay was simply to write a personal statement on anything we would like the admissions committee to consider. I decided that committee members probably grow weary of endless essays pontificating the virtues of their writers, so I just shared something about myself and my past."

In the summer of 1990 my father, a mechanic for the city of Grand Junction, Colorado, was involved in an accident. He was working on a fire truck engine when his hand glanced too close to the turbocharger. The screen that should have acted as a barrier to such accidents was missing, and a large portion of my father's right hand was instantly consumed. A small financial settlement was made, but it did not correspond to the resulting pain which even now remains present or to the loss of one's sole trade.

Within a few months my father found a job as an auto-electric rebuilder. This was a step down for a master mechanic, but the position was less physically demanding; besides, employment opportunities in Grand Junction were rare. A year and a half later, my father invested everything he owned into his own auto-electric business, Mesa Alternator Service.

My father, mother, eldest brother, and I all worked together at the small shop. I did everything from filing taxes to polishing parts with a bead-blaster. My mother and I spent weekends writing up advertisements, mailing out statements, and tidying up the shop. My father himself worked seventeen-hour days and developed alternators and starters vastly superior to those already on the market. The business was wildly successful; it was out of the red within the first year, and profits rose steadily each subsequent year.

People often tell my father that he has been extraordinarily lucky; I disagree. The individuals involved with the operation of that company sacrificed to ensure its success. The same people often remark that I, a first generation college student, have also been extraordinarily lucky to attend such fine institutions. I have enjoyed many educational experiences during these past years; yet it must be emphasized that I approached them determined to use every method of succeeding. The experience I gained at Mesa Alternator Service facilitated this greatly; when I found it necessary to work full-time while in school, I was able to persuade a company to hire me despite a policy not to hire full-time students. They did not regret their decision.

I have often read that the greatest predictor of success in an academic setting results from growing up in a family with strong educational and professional backgrounds. I suppose this is true to a certain extent, especially in respect to professional programs. Yet a far more important determinant of success is to take measure of how the student resolves to put to use all the resources available at the time. My GPA and LSAT score indicate that I have the potential to succeed at law school. The short chapter of family history recounted above shows why I believe that intelligent resolve to succeed may count for more.

Daniel Martin

Dan lived or traveled abroad during most of his post-college years, visiting more than twenty countries and studying several languages. He started his own company in Japan, backpacked around Asia for two years, and enrolled in a Chinese university to study Mandarin before coming back to start law school.

Stats:

LSAT: 173

GPA: 3.14 (sociology)

College attended: State University of New York—College at Geneseo

Class: 1995

Hometown: Liverpool, NY

Gender: Male

Race: White (though Daniel "always checked the 'decline to answer' ethnicity box" on his law school applications)

Law school attending: University of Michigan Law School

Class: 2005

Applied to the following law schools:

Accepted: University of Michigan

Denied: Columbia, Harvard, University of Virginia, Yale

Other: Duke University, University of Chicago, Vanderbilt (placed on waitlist by all)

Personal statement:

(From the University of Michigan Law School's application)

"Michigan's talented student body is one of the Law School's richest resources. Each entering class of Michigan law students is composed of exceptionally accomplished people who bring a vast spectrum of experiences and perspectives to the Law School community. To aid in constructing such a diverse and interesting class, Michigan's application for admission requires a personal statement. This statement provides applicants an opportunity to demonstrate the ways in which they can contribute their unique talents and experiences to the Law School.

"The required personal statement should be well organized and well written; apart from that, the form and content are up to you. Successful applicants have elaborated on significant personal, academic, and professional experiences, as well as meaningful intellectual interests and extracurricular activities. In general, the personal statement should not be a mere catalog of accomplishments and activities, but a thoughtful explanation of what those accomplishments and activities have meant to you.

"Applicants are also invited to submit, at their discretion, two additional 250-word essays.... The second optional essay should reveal, in a way that an LSAT score or a grade point average cannot, something about the way you think. For example, you might choose to discuss an intellectual or social problem you have faced or a book or film that has particularly affected you."

(Daniel used the following statement in all of the law school applications he submitted in 2002.)

"I'd like to see the world, for the whirligig of men is, as it were, a living book and as good as any science."

-Gogol, Dead Souls

I remember the day clearly—it was day number six of an eleven-day Vipassana ("Insight") silent meditation course in Dharamsala, a Tibetan refugee village in Northern India—after some fifty hours of meditation, six days since my last spoken words, I decided that I was ready to go to law school. Hundreds of monkeys screamed in the trees above me, and the sky was ethereally blue.

I left the US over a year ago, to travel throughout much of Asia, in search of adventure, a bevy of unpredictable experiences, and insights into a world of multifarious ideals—I have encountered all three on various levels. But while traveling has had innumerable benefits to me as an investment in my future self— challenging many of my opinions and world-views—I am now ready to begin my career, among some of the world's brightest objective thinkers.

Because my ideas and plans have changed so frequently over the past six years, I am not sure where my career will lead; I would like to work internationally, perhaps serving as a corporate liaison between cultures. A law school education will open many doors, but I am most interested in interacting with intelligent peers, and learning how to improve my ability to think objectively on a number of levels.

My strong interest in objective analyses first manifested itself two years ago, in thoughts and discussions about reading. I was working as a night security guard at a public nursing home—since most of the residents posed only a minimal flight risk in the middle of the night, and the building was equipped with a state-of-the-art security system to thwart unauthorized entry, my official duties were few. I am grateful for my curious younger self's vigilance in performing a self-imposed duty: reading widely, across disciplines. An average of five hours per night, I read mostly academic journals or textbooks, spending roughly equal time studying neuro-science, genetics, sociology, philosophy, psychology and literature. I would read three books at a time, so as to spot patterns and similarities in the different fields.

In the last year, I have read countless books on innumerable bus journeys or train rides, and held many interesting conversations with people from many countries. I have learned the worth and the sacrifices inherent in probing the minds or hearts of people from different cultures. I will bring a valuable form of diversity to law school, in my exposure to different cultures and the perspective which objective analysis of my experiences has given me. I have spent four of the past five years abroad, visiting thirty countries. But I was not always reading a book or debating the nature of dreams or emotions while I was riding buses or trains...

In Laos, fate put me on a truck with no headlights, driving slowly up a mountain dirt road after five days of monsoon rain—after a flat tire, several hours of slogging through mud, and a brake problem, I found myself sitting on the roof of the cab with a Vietnamese man, illuminating the road with our flashlights so the driver could see it. In Indonesia I woke up at 2am on an overnight bus to find a machine gun in my face—all of the other men had been taken off the bus. It turned out to be a standard military checkpost in an unstable region—after showing my passport to the soldier and trying to explain in Indonesian that my visa was not expired, I went back to sleep.

My serious interest in travel was born shortly after I moved to Tokyo in 1996. Japan is a fun place, full of mysteries and the strange idiosyncratic trends of 110 million people. I was a conversational English teacher for a year, and I left that job to start my own company—my company was very small, as I was the only employee! I was an English Consultant for Hikari Tsushin, Inc., a mid-size telecommunications distributor—as such, my duties were "anything and every-thing related to English," including Business English lessons to executives; "Sur-vival English crash courses" for Directors and the President; and writing English public relations materials, such as a bond underwriting proposal or the annual report.

In Japan I met many travelers on their way around the world—it was primarily their stories which peaked my interest, convincing me to leave Japan in search of self-education and funny stories. One of my most surprising yet disturbing lessons learned is that much of the rest of the world's people understand America and American interests, at times quite intimately. I have had discussions on American politics in the jungles of Sumatra, small villages in Northern Thailand, and in the mountains of Nepal. Our overall lack of knowledge about the rest of the world is a dangerous vulnerability which, in my opinion, needs to be addressed. Though budget traveling around the world does not pay the bills, and entails many emotional sacrifices, I honestly feel that I am a better person because of my experiences. I feel that I would be a valuable member of your entering class, and I respectfully hope that you concur.

Optional essay number two:

(Submitted for Michigan's application)

Culmination of Research, Travel and Thought, 1996-2001

"Through conscious beings the universe has generated self-awareness."

-V.S. Ramachandran

Humankind is an eyeball, which perceives itself through the lens of its internally generated conception of a self-image.

The human body is a complex jumble of incalculable intricacy, housing untold numbers of competing desires, thoughts, proteins and parasites, imprisoned together in the dense jungle of Self. Our memories, antibodies, dreams and genes lay the groundwork while our consciousness forges the path, examining detailed interpretations of the present course.

Similarly, every human society is composed of competing, yet symbiotic, cells and organs: its members and the institutions to which they relate. All human cultures, through the actions of their members, effectively promote or discourage certain behaviors, emotional states, and family structures, in line with a core set of values and ideas through which they are defined at the macro level. Most societies, like all organisms, seek to reproduce and expand their influence.

How cultures interact with one another, how people within a given society interact, and how the individual cells and desires within those people do the same, is the essence of the study of people—one of my core interests—an integration of the fields of biology, neuroscience, psychology, philosophy, physics, religion, anthropology, sociology, and laws which unite, divide, and define them.

Going one step further, I believe that the Earth is alive, and that a diverse humankind is one of its most important organs—taken as a whole, we are the self—conscious mind struggling to understand its place in the universe, the organ of planetary self-awareness.

Previous attempts at law school:

In 2001, Daniel applied to Yale alone with an LSAT score of 170. He was denied admission.

In 1997, he applied to Columbia, Harvard, NYU, Stanford, University of Chicago, University of Michigan, University of Pennsylvania, Vanderbilt, and Yale.

Columbia, NYU, Harvard, Stanford, University of Chicago, University of Michigan, and Yale denied him admission. He was placed on the waitlists of Vanderbilt and University of Pennsylvania.

University of Pennsylvania Law School

Elizabeth Horowitz

Elizabeth graduated magna cum laude after being placed on the Dean's List every semester at Tufts. She was also a four-year starter on the Tufts University varsity women's lacrosse team, and her teammates elected her captain her senior year. That same year, she also led a seminar for freshmen and acted as a peer advisor to the fourteen students in the class. She has worked in a law office for the past few summers.

Stats:
LSAT: 168
GPA: 3.63 (child development)
College attended: Tufts University
Class: 2002
Hometown: Westbury, NY
Gender: Female
Race: White
Law school attending: University of Pennsylvania Law School
Class: 2006

Applied to the following law schools:
Accepted: Boston University, Fordham, Georgetown, University of Pennsylvania
Denied: Columbia (after being placed on waitlist), Harvard, NYU
Other: None

Personal statements:
(For Columbia, Georgetown, Fordham, and NYU)
According to Elizabeth, "Basically, these schools requested that you simply share any information that might help them to make their decisions."

People, for the most part, can be divided into two groups – chocolate people and vanilla people. You may find an occasional strawberry but they are rare and, for the most part, unheard of. I am, without a doubt, a chocolate person. Be it ice cream, candy, or cake, I always opt for the chocolate choice.

I inherited this preference from my father, who suffers from a slight obsession with the flavor. My mother is quite the opposite; her loyalties lie with vanilla. I suppose that the chocolate-lover's gene is dominant. My passion for the flavor, however, is not solely a result of my genealogy. My ever-so-dedicated father has always been a source of encouragement regarding the pursuit of my interests, and the development of my sweet tooth was no exception.

My mother always worked during the day, but for a time during my grade school years she had to work one night during the week as well. My older brother and I were left in the hands of my less than health conscious father. Maintaining our balanced diets of three squares a day had always been my mother's terrain. With my father treading upon it, however, it was not long before "Mom's Work Night" was transformed into "Chocolate Night."

My mother would leave for the office and my brother and I would anxiously wait to hear my father's key turn in the lock. We were always prepared, having cleaned off the coffee table in the den to make room for the pile of sweets he would bring. I remember climbing up onto the counters, searching the cupboards for the tallest glass I could find. (I never checked the sink; washing a dish wasn't an option.) I would fill the glass until it was brimming with milk, threatening an overflow at the slightest disturbance. After all, there was nothing worse than having to go upstairs for a milk refill while my selfish brother continued to greedily eat in my absence. Once filled up with my dairy fuel, I would slowly make my way down the den stairs, where I would sit in anxious anticipation of my father's arrival.

Finally, he would appear! After putting down his briefcase and taking off his coat, he would descend the stairs with the treasures of the night tucked under his arm in a brown paper bag. One by one, he would take out the assortment of savory sweets. The exotic bars always impressed me, or at least, at the time, I thought they were exotic. These were not the everyday Hershey Bars and Baby Ruths that I was used to buying with my left over lunch money. These curious candies had names I could not even pronounce; we feasted on Toblerone, Godiva and Bacci – this was classy stuff.

So, with a fleeting glimpse of the stomachache that was sure to follow, Chocolate Night began. While trying to ration my milk, I proceeded to eat an obscene and downright unhealthy amount of chocolate. My father would tell us facts about each bar, where it came from, and what made it unique, most of which I don't remember. What I do remember, however, is the weekly tradition that we created. I remember looking forward not only to the appeasement of my confectionery cravings, but also to the time I spent with my greedy older brother and my hardworking father. Don't misunderstand me, the chocolate was a plus. In reality, though, it was merely a vehicle that my father used to bring us together around the coffee table; to bring us together at all. While fostering my growing sweet tooth, he fostered sweet memories as well.

I can also recall, quite vividly, the feeling of contentment that consumed me (no pun intended) while we sat on the rug, chewing on our chocolate treats. I felt whole, as if I belonged nowhere else but in that spot, milk in hand and chocolate in mouth.

It was that same feeling that motivated me to apply to law school. My father claims that he knew it all along and he was just waiting for me to figure it out for myself. In the end, however, it was that perfect-fit-feeling that made my decision so clear. Opting for law school felt as natural as opting for rocky road over butter pecan. The thought of pursuing a career in law stirs the same sense of completeness that I felt while sitting around the coffee table. Though I'm not sure how law school will measure up to Chocolate Night, I am expecting great things, and I know I will not be disappointed. Chocolate night always left me feeling full and contented; I expect that after digesting my education in law, I will feel quite the same.

(For Boston University, Harvard, and University of Pennsylvania)
"What academic and/or personal reasons caused you to apply to law school?"

Law is my career of choice, but this was not always the case. I must admit that if five years ago someone had told me I would one day go to law school I would have declared them completely insane. My interest emerged over time, through exposure to law-related courses and relationships with people involved in the profession. It grew slowly and steadily until I realized that pursuing a career in law was exactly what I wanted to do.

While in high school, I took a forensics and criminology class, which initially piqued my interest in the field of law. There, I studied court procedures and spent a lot of time developing and performing mock trials. Besides being intrigued by the system of law itself, the contemplative reasoning involved in developing and presenting a case was a rewarding challenge.

The class truly engaged me, or at least the criminology aspects of it did. (Finding fingerprints and deducing blood spurt angles were not quite as appealing.) However, it was not until my junior year of college that I seriously considered pursuing law as a profession. During my spring semester, I took a course concentrating on educational law and children's advocacy. It quickly became my favorite class. I found pleasure in reading Supreme Court cases and learning about the law in a more intimate and explicit way.

My interest was sparked and I began to contemplate law as a career. However, before making any life-altering decisions, a bit of experience was needed. I spent the summer working for Joel S. Kaplan, an attorney with a private practice in Garden City, New York. I worked as an assistant with a paralegal. Though my duties were mainly clerical, I was exposed to a variety of cases and to the workings of a law office. Mr. Kaplan would kindly take time from his busy day to discuss with me the procedures and details of specific cases. By summer's end, my mind was made up; law was to be my choice of vocation.

Aside from my academic and work-related experience, it is my natural disposition that suits me for the field of law. My father describes this as my "Type A personality," which he comments on every time I happen to disagree with him. I welcome the debate of controversial topics and often prefer to argue against what I believe; this allows me to examine and to enlightenment myself to opposing points of view.

It may have been a gradual process, but now the decision has been made, and my pursuit of a career in law has begun. I am on my way, and my confidence in my abilities will keep me focused on continuing my stride, and will propel me to my chosen destination.

Ashley Street

Ashley's primary extracurricular activity was a local pre-law fraternity, Beta Alpha Rho, in which she was an officer for two semesters. She was also a member of Alpha Phi Sorority and competed in mock trial tournaments. She held part-time jobs as a messenger for the Texas State Senate during her junior year and as a Felony Court clerk during her senior year. She also worked as a summer intern with the Bush for President Campaign. She worked as a community supervision (probation) officer for Travis County after her graduation from UT and attends the University of Texas School of Law.

Stats:

LSAT: 179
GPA: 3.63
College attended: University of Texas—Austin
Class: 2001
Hometown: Albuquerque, NM
Gender: Female
Race: White
Law school attending: University of Texas School of Law
Class: 2005

Applied to the following law schools:

> **Accepted:** NYU, University of Southern California, University of Texas
> **Denied:** Stanford
> **Other:** None

Personal statement:

Ashley recalls the crux of the essay prompt as "Your personal statement should give the admissions committee insight to your character and experiences."

My grandfather passed away during my sophomore year of high school. Oddly, the one thing I remember clearly about his passing is writing the obituary. As my mother and I sat and tried to write a statement that could sum up my grandpa's seventy years on earth in fifty words or less, we could not think of the words to describe the adversity he had overcome in his lifetime. Grandpa was survived by seven children and twenty grandchildren, of which I was the youngest. As a child, I looked up to my grandpa more than anyone else, and I admired his courage. I was *his* baby girl.

To this day, no one in our family really knows where our family came from. Grandpa worked in the coal mines as a child alongside his father. When he was thirteen years old, the mine collapsed killing his father, my great-grandfather. Shortly thereafter, my great grandmother abandoned her children. She left my grandpa, as the eldest child, to raise the others. Grandpa refused to talk about his mother. The only thing he would ever say was that she was an "ole' Indian squaw." Because he had to raise his brothers and sisters, grandpa received little formal education; yet, he eventually would own his own landscaping business. I respect my grandpa's adaptability and resourcefulness. He never had a lot of money, nor did my parents when I was young, but I never knew that because they always made sure I had whatever I needed to succeed. They were never afraid, or at least they did not show it. Their courage is something I respect, envy and strive to emulate.

As mentioned earlier, my grandpa was survived by twenty-seven people. Among all twenty-seven plus my dad's family, I am the first to graduate from college. I am certainly the first to pursue a graduate degree. Being the first has its advantages and disadvantages. One definite advantage is that whenever I accomplish something new, whether it is making the dean's list or getting an internship, my family is excessively proud. Also, I have never been pressured to follow someone else's path. I am free to pursue my own goals and interests and no one else can judge me or claim that they did it better. On the down side, my entire college career has been filled with unknowns. I feel like I am constantly walking in shadows. In *The Hollow Man,* T.S. Elliot wrote "Between the idea/ And the reality / Between the motion/ And the Act/ Falls the Shadow." It is that shadow, that unknown which is the biggest obstacle I faced when applying to college, during my undergraduate years and now applying to law school.

I began noticing the difficulty of being the first when I started applying to undergraduate programs. Neither my parents, nor anyone else I knew had gone through that process before, so they were unable to offer much advice. To make things more confusing, I moved from Texas to New Mexico during my junior year. My counselors did not know me well, and I did not feel comfortable asking teachers I had only known for a semester for recommendations. While filling out the applications I was a nervous wreck. I had never even heard of a personal statement before and did not know how to go about trying to actually write one. Throughout college I had other similar experiences. I was moving hundreds of miles from my parents, and I did not even know where I was going to live until three weeks before I moved to Austin. I was not aware you had to apply for on campus housing before you were even accepted to the University. Once classes started, I felt all alone at a very large school, so I decided to become involved in some student organizations. I quickly went from knowing no one to feeling like the campus had 5,000 students instead of 50,000. After four years, I finally graduated. Preparing for graduation was stressful. One of the best parts of my life was coming to an end. I had more family in town than most of my friends because everyone was so excited for me. The actual day of graduation was both stressful and wonderful, because I was the first.

I love having the recognition of being the first to do something, yet it often makes me feel pressured. I know my family is counting on me to succeed and to make the most of the opportunities I have been blessed with. However, I know my grandpa is always watching over me and guiding me wherever I may go. He always knew that I would excel at whatever I tried to do and was always encouraging. Although the challenges I face are nothing in comparison to the hardships of his life, I know he would be proud that I graduated from college and even happier to hear that I am going to go to law school. After all, he was the one who always told me I argued too much.

After law school, I hope to use my degrees and talents to continue stretching the boundaries. After working with the Travis County Felony Courts, I have decided to pursue a career in criminal justice. When I was younger I wanted to be the first female Attorney General. Janet Reno beat me to it, but there is always something new to accomplish. The most important thing I have learned in college is to always push myself. If I would have followed the easy road or only done the bare minimum, I would never have accomplished all that I have. I thank my Grandpa and my parents for teaching me that and demonstrating the courage that it takes to achieve more than what is expected.

Anonymous

Anonymous ran on the varsity track and field team in college and performed service work during her undergraduate years, including a summer internship at the Boys and Girls Club. She worked for two years as a technical consultant for Accenture before attending law school.

Stats:
  LSAT: 172
  GPA: 3.8 (mathematics and philosophy)
  College attended: University of Notre Dame
  Class: 2000
  Hometown: Lakeville, IN
  Gender: Female
  Race: White
  Law school attending: University of Virginia School of Law
  Class: 2005

Applied to the following law schools:
  Accepted: Georgetown, Northwestern, Notre Dame, NYU, University of Chicago
  Denied: None
  Other: None

Personal statement:

In Anonymous's words, "The questions on all the applications were basically 'Please tell us about yourself, your experiences, and qualities that make you a good candidate for studying law.'"

I would never have thought that West Virginia politics could be so exciting. During my senior year of college, I visited Charleston, the state capital, as part of a one-week "social immersion experience." My fellow students and I learned first-hand about the mining practice of mountaintop removal and the devastation that this practice causes in the topography, water supply, and homes of those living near mining sites. On one busy day, my group visited a mining site, spoke with the Secretary of State, met with a regional activist group, and even appeared on the local news to comment on that day's landmark judicial decision to prohibit coal miners from burying state streams. It was an exciting experience because I had the opportunity to study a single issue from all of its legal, social, economic, environmental, and personal perspectives.

This experience was one of many that piqued my interest in the legal profession. But why should I necessarily pursue a career in law? I could work in business, academia, or the nonprofit arenas. During my Appalachian immersion experience, I had met with people who worked in each of these areas, citizens who were, in their own ways, seeking to improve the social and economic situations around them.

One of my motivations for choosing law is well expressed in a statement made by Jeff Allen, a West Virginia environmental activist/preacher who has battled with the mining industry in his home state his entire life. We discussed my interest in law one day on a visit to the local Home Depot, picking up lumber for a mobile home that my group was repairing from flood damage caused by mining. He commented: "What all of us really need is people to help make our case, people who can understand the legal arguments against mountaintop removal while not losing sight of those that it affects."

Practicing law requires becoming entangled in human problems and looking for often less than perfect human solutions. It demands compromise and diligence. Often, lawyers are called upon to combine the expertise of economists, sociologists, volunteers and other social experts. At their best, lawyers *don't* lose sight of the persons that their work is affecting. And, as a lawyer, I won't necessarily need to practice environmental law to face these kinds of compelling and difficult issues.

I chose to delay pursuing law as a career after I graduated. I did so because I felt that I could gain a wide range of skills in the workplace, skills that complemented my undergraduate degree. My post-graduation work experience has offered me an intense introduction to the business and professional worlds. I was required to quickly learn an entirely new field, including mastering technical, managerial, and social skills. On a daily basis, I work to integrate requests from multiple parties to arrive at viable solutions to problems. I independently manage others in a multicultural setting. These are all skills that can be useful in the field of law. My conversations with those who practice law have cemented my decision that it is the career choice for me.

Although I am proud of my academic and professional record, I believe that it is my character that makes me especially well suited to a career in law. I have always welcomed the challenges of interdisciplinary studies. Further, I have sought to use my talents for the benefit and empowerment of those around me. I feel that this natural curiosity and compassion for others would lead to a successful learning experience for me at *<<Insert Law School>>*'s School of Law.

David Greene

David served as the president of the Kite and Key Society at the University of Pennsylvania, the school's oldest and largest student group. He was also elected to the Undergraduate Assembly, Penn's student government. He performed research in psychiatry and political science during the summer after his junior year. David graduated with a double major in political science and engineering in 2002.

Stats:

LSAT: 164
GPA: 3.69 (political science and engineering)
College attended: University of Pennsylvania
Class: 2002
Hometown: Newtown, PA
Gender: Male
Race: White
Law school attending: University of Virginia School of Law
Class: 2005

Applied to the following law schools:

Accepted: George Washington University (with one-third scholarship), Northwestern, University of Virginia
Denied: Columbia, Harvard, NYU
Other: Georgetown, University of Pennsylvania (placed on waitlist by both)

Personal statement:

David did not write his personal statement in response to a specific prompt.

I was commanded to walk quickly and keep my arms at my sides. Any sudden movements may evoke agitation from the patients, I was told. I followed a few steps behind my advisor, unsure what to expect as he pushed open the doors leading to the clinic. On my first day with the Unit for Experimental Psychiatry, I found myself in the psych ward at the Hospital of the University of Pennsylvania.

I had expected to work in a computer lab crunching numbers for my independent research; instead, I observed institutionalized patients who were spending weeks in the ward. I investigated a typical lab where a patient would be deprived of sleep in order to test reaction times at various levels of sleeplessness. My study, along with other work in the lab, would benefit NASA and the armed forces; astronauts and soldiers receive only six hours of sleep per night on average, and my results, part of a long-term project, would help determine if such limited hours would reduce their performance.

My first attempt at independent research involved writing an original computer program analyzing over one million points of data, and I found the task daunting. Facing the prospect of putting together over one thousand lines of computer code required me to find new approaches to intricate problems. The only way I could begin to tackle the project involved breaking the complex end-task into a number of smaller, easier-to-obtain goals that I could manage individually.

My work in the Unit for Experimental Psychiatry ward taught me valuable problem solving skills. I believe that both my engineering education and my experience applying it to research will prove valuable in the study and practice of law. Both research questions and legal problems have numerous possible answers, and choosing the proper initial course for my research showed me all the directions in which it could progress. In my study, I had many options for a number of variables: What computing language should I use? How should I structure the program? When I wrote guest opinion pieces arguing on behalf of social and political issues in the University of Pennsylvania's student newspaper, I had to carefully construct a logical argument using relevant information to support my point of view. My analytical ability, developed through an engineering education and improved through practical applications, will be helpful in a legal career.

My experience with the Unit of Experimental Psychiatry was a lesson in "crash courses:" first, how to walk through the Psych ward safely, and, secondly, how to work, define, and eventually solve a complex problem. While I do not expect a legal career will require the first skill I learned through my research, I feel confident that I will benefit from the problem-solving skills I acquired as I study and eventually practice law in ideally a business or technological setting.

Anonymous

After graduating from the University of Chicago, Anonymous returned to his hometown and worked for two years as a technical writer. He then enrolled in journalism school at the University of Oregon, graduating in 1998. He was granted membership in the national honor society Kappa Tau Alpha. He worked briefly during journalism school as an associate editor for a trade magazine and, after graduating, as an editor for a small publisher of financial books and periodicals.

Stats:
LSAT: 164
GPA: 3.1, master's degree, 3.9
College attended: University of Chicago; master's in journalism, University of Oregon
Class: 1995; master's degree, 1998
Hometown: Eugene, OR
Gender: Male
Race: White
Law school attending: Vanderbilt University Law School
Class: 2005

Applied to the following law schools:
Accepted: Case Western University, Emory, Tulane, University of Oregon, Vanderbilt
Denied: Duke, Notre Dame, University of Virginia
Other: College of William and Mary, Washington and Lee, Washington University in St. Louis (placed on waitlist by all)

Personal statement:
Anonymous did not write his personal statement for any specific prompt.

Question: "What do you get when you cross the Godfather with a lawyer?"

Answer: "An offer you can't understand."

It is perhaps impertinent of me to begin my personal statement with a joke about lawyers, But I do so to illustrate an important point: most students begin law school woefully unprepared for training in legal writing, having little knowledge of English grammar, correct usage, and proper style. And after three years of reading convoluted opinions and statutes, most of these students finish law school with the notion that good legal writing requires an impenetrable, jargon-filled style.

I came across a fine example of this recently. An oversight committee in Maryland, charged with the unenviable task of interpreting many of that state's more perplexing statutes, came across this monstrosity:

> The Board may appoint, discharge at pleasure, and fix the compensation of the secretary and such clerical force as from time to time in its judgment may be necessary in the administration of this subtitle if it has funds available for the payment of such persons.

("It means" said the committee, "that the Board may employ a staff in accordance with the state budget.") It seems that impenetrable writing is not just common in the legal profession, but a requirement. I recently saw an advertisement placed by a business law journal seeking applicants able, in part, to "produce verbose, 1st-draft material under tight deadlines"!

I can tell you that professional writers in the field in which I work—stock and commodity market investment—labor under the same delusions. I see it every day in my job as an editor. Recently, my company's lead writer—a New York University graduate with nearly 20 years of experience—handed me his latest article to edit. I turned his three pages of convoluted, wordy prose into less than a page of lucid, concise writing. When I presented him with the edited version, his complaint was immediate: "The article sounds far less impressive the way you have it written." I asked him to provide me with an example. He pointed to one of his original sentences, which he was quite proud of(!): "Prognostications of prominent investment-house analysts and other well-known pontificators provides an ominous picture for the stock market's future, making it less inviting than bonds." "Here," he said, "is a sentence that *sounds* important—one that immediately grabs the reader's attention and holds it firmly."

This all-too-common misjudgment among writers—and the source of most bad writing, I believe—is the *desire to impress* the reader combined with the writer's *dearth of literacy.* This was the case here: the former was apparent in the writer's complaint to me; the latter was evident in the original sentence:

GRAMMAR ERROR: In English, particularizing expressions with *of* express a partitive (possessive) meaning and require a defining word—in this case, the definite article *The* should be used.

USAGE ERROR: A *pontificator* does not offer predictions (the intended meaning) but rather expresses opinions in a pompous or dogmatic way.

Prognostications of prominent investment-house analysts and other well-known pontificators provides an ominous picture for the stock market's future, making it less inviting than bonds.

USAGE ERROR: You provide a picture *for* someone; you provide a picture *of* something.

GRAMMAR ERROR: The compound adjective *stock market's* cannot serve as the antecedent of the pronoun *it*—a noun is required.

GRAMMAR ERROR: The plural subject *Prognosticatic* requires a plural verb—*prov*

When I pointed out to my friend just some of the errors in this sentence, his confidence in its virtues vanished. He agreed that my edited sentence—"Many analysts predict a general decline in the stock markets; if these analysts are correct, the bond markets will rise"—was better.

I am not suggesting that highly literate writers always write well or that grammatical prose is invariably well-written. To write well requires a *high degree of literacy* and *good judgment about the written word.* Much of the strength of my candidacy for admission to Vanderbilt Law School lies in the fact that, as a skilled and experienced writer and editor, I have both: I achieved a high degree of literacy by earning a two-year journalism degree (and graduating at the top of my class); I attained good judgement about the written word by working for two years as a technical writer and five years as an editor. My knowledge and experience in this area, combined with the education I received at the University of Chicago, provide strong evidence of my ability to succeed at the study and practice of law.

Bryan Ketroser

Bryan completed an internship with the housing unit of a legal services agency in his senior year. While Bryan worked in the cafeteria part-time during his first year, as a Japanese language tutor part-time during his second and third years, and as a temp full-time during the summers, he had no extracurricular activities save the occasional game of tennis or chess with a friend.

Stats:

LSAT: 180

GPA: 3.89 (East Asian studies and linguistics)

College attended: Brandeis University

Class: 2002

Hometown: Minnetonka, MN

Gender: Male

Race: White

Law school attending: Yale Law School

Class: 2005

Applied to the following law schools:

Accepted: Harvard, University of California—Berkeley (Boalt), University of Chicago, Yale

Denied: Stanford (according to Bryan, "waitlisted into oblivion, actually")

Other: None

Personal statement:

Bryan's "personal statement was not tailored to the individual law schools; they all got the same thing."

Determination. If you are truly interested in my personality, there it is. This is not to say there is nothing else to me, it is just that determination is what seems to stick out most. Nor is it to say I am a perfectionist. Perfectionism places too much emphasis on results, at the expense of the process. I always strive for the best possible outcome because it is the best way to enjoy the journey, not just because it leads to better results (though, of course, this is a perk).

Oddly, this has a great deal to do with a disorder I only began to understand at the age of fourteen. Around that time, friends and teachers began commenting on facial twitches that I was exhibiting with increasing frequency. I had coped with minor tics so long that, by then, I was only vaguely aware of their existence. But then they started getting worse, forcing my consciousness to deal with them. My father – ironically, a neurologist – gave me his diagnosis: Tourettes Syndrome. This was soon confirmed by another physician.

The symptoms are primarily a collection of omnipresent and ever-changing tics. It is difficult to adequately explain what a tic feels like to one who has never experienced it, but if the reader has not had the "pleasure," the best analogue would be to imagine having an itch. While no actual feeling of skin irritation accompanies a tic, the impulse which leads to a tic is much akin to feeling the need to scratch an itch.

My case of Tourettes has been neither so mild as to be readily ignored nor, in my opinion, so severe as to warrant medication. But no matter where I go or what I do, it is always in at least one corner of my mind, for like the urge to scratch an itch, it *is* possible to suppress a tic. Learning to live with Tourettes has thus helped me in two ways. First, it has taught me patience; tics are constantly waxing and waning, and when they are bad, they have a tendency to require more attention to maintain the same level of control. This generally becomes aggravating, which in turn worsens the tics. The only way to avoid such a cycle is by being patient, and not letting the extra difficulty get to you. The other thing I have gained from the disorder is, as I mentioned before, an aversion to giving up. Tourettes is with me 24/7 and, while I pause every now and then to think how fortunate I am that I did not get a more disabling version, it is something that requires constant effort.

One of the first tests of my patience and resolve presented itself during my final year of middle school. I had been moderately overweight for several years, but as I grew older I began crossing the line distinguishing "chubby" from "obese." At around 5'6", my weight had crept up to over 180 pounds, and was still rising. My parents occasionally suggested that I take steps to lose the weight, but I hated exercise, and one can no doubt imagine just how thrilled the average 12 or 13 year-old boy would be to go on a diet. I was aware of the problem, but uninterested in putting forth the effort needed to rectify it.

And then, it happened. At some point, I just said to myself, "I know I can do it, so why in the world *haven't* I?" I have been a different person ever since. On the spot,

I resolved to lose weight. I played tennis virtually every day during the spring and summer, and in the months I could not play, I used a treadmill. Perhaps more importantly, I forever changed my eating habits. The changes were difficult; there were many days when I spent two hours on the treadmill, only to sit down to a dinner that was considerably smaller (and greener) than my body desired. Still, I never questioned my decision to stick with it. Completion of the task was simply a given. Within nine months, I shrank from over 180 pounds to an even 140 pounds. By consistently making the right dietary choices and getting enough exercise, I have stayed between 140 and 145 pounds for the past seven years.

I have also harnessed my determination when it comes to my academic interests. A fascination with the people and culture of Japan led to my enrollment in an intensive Japanese language summer program at the University of Minnesota at the end of my junior year of high school. In eight weeks, I learned the equivalent of a year's worth of Japanese. Whereas seven years of Spanish classes had me doubting my foreign language-learning abilities, those eight weeks showed me that I could succeed in even my weakest areas if I put my mind to it. And put my mind to it I did. The class met for five hours a day (in addition to over an hour of commuting time), Monday through Friday, and often required another five hours of homework or more per night. The first surprise was that I was doing well, but the big surprise was that I was having the time of my life. Throughout my college career, I made certain that I put this level of determination into all my academic endeavors, and found that it invariably lead to greater enjoyment of each and every one. The fact that law is my chief interest will be the supreme bonus in the three years to come, and this makes me even more excited to dive headfirst into the law school experience.

As for Japanese, I continued my studies throughout my senior year of high school, taking evening classes at the University of Minnesota after my high school classes. I went to Japan for six weeks the summer preceding my matriculation at Brandeis University, then continued to study the language both there and at nearby Wellesley College. I am currently translating the second of two short stories from Japanese into English for an honors thesis in East Asian Studies. And I'm loving every minute of it.

Anonymous

Anonymous grew up in Washington, D.C., and graduated from the Sidwell Friends School, a private lower and upper school in the District. She studied musicology at the University of Chicago and graduated in three years, receiving both general and departmental honors. She spent six years preparing for a career as an opera singer, studying in New York and Italy. She then decided to do something different—at least for a while. Ultimately, rather than going to law school, even though she was accepted to two of the most prestigious and selective schools in the nation, she is pursuing a Ph.D. in policy analysis at the RAND Graduate School.

Stats:

LSAT: 173

GPA: 3.55 (musicology)

College attended: University of Chicago

Class: 1996

Hometown: Washington, DC

Gender: Female

Race: White

Law school attending: Anonymous chose not to attend law school.

Class: None

Applied to the following law schools:

Accepted: Columbia, NYU

Denied: Harvard, Yale

Other: University of Chicago (placed on waitlist)

Personal statement:

In Anonymous's words, "The essay prompt was, for all of my applications, a vague question that boiled down to 'What would you like us to know about you?' For schools that asked specifically why them, I added a paragraph at the end of the essay."

The idea of my going to law school is a new one, but it is settling on me nicely. It feels somewhat like finding shoes that fit well—an exquisite relief. And like new shoes, law school will not dictate the path I take, but it will make the walking easier and allow for a journey with more interesting terrain.

Until recently I was training for a career as an opera singer. I was determined to be one who survives the brutal process to become a well-respected, well-paid performer. But then I realized that this single-minded pursuit of my goal was making it impossible for me to reach it. I had been assuming the best way to become a great singer is to cut off any serious exploration of other interests and to put all of my energies into singing. But expertise is not a zero-sum game. Gain in one area does not imply a loss in another—quite the opposite, in fact. While I was starving most of my interests with the hope of freeing up nutrients to nourish one, my singing got caught in the general blight. For me to sing at all, I need to let my career aspirations go and let my voice find its own way on its own time.

So then what next? It has been an exhilarating process to find an answer. For the first time I have no preconceived idea of what my next step will be—I am considering all options. Suddenly the interesting things I pass by have become tantalizing possibilities. I used to regret not going to a music conservatory. That is no longer true. I am once again glad I had the opportunity to wallow in the intellectual excitement that pervades the air at the University of Chicago. Now I can feel free to take sculpting and math and emergency medicine classes along with my weekly voice coachings.

I have worked off and on for a woman who lives in my building and owns a catering company. My favorite job for her was serving at a Christmas party a year ago at the American consulate to the UN. The snippets of conversation I caught while passing hors d'oeuvres left me stimulated for days: an American talking with an African about how the CIA had been worried that a quiet coup had been taking place in the African's country until they realized that it was AIDS not rebels killing off government officials; Kofi Annan wishing Richard Holbrooke a merry Christmas; others gossiping about the fickleness of money and power. It did not cross my mind to dream of one day having access to a room like that without a shrimp plate in my hand. I am dreaming now.

A little over a year ago, I took a part-time job teaching for Princeton Review. I applied for the job because I had heard it was well paying, flexible, and somewhat interesting. It quickly became a passion. I have become smitten with these tests, most particularly with the GMAT, my first love, and the LSAT, a much more recent acquaintance. The two tests are very different in nature—the GMAT is sneaky and the LSAT exacting—but both require a distilled form of problem solving. The content has reawakened my interest in mathematics and logic. In formulating the best strategy to approach the test questions, I have learned much about the psychology of decision-making that is so integral to the way the questions are structured and the incorrect answers are written. The tests also demand precise thinking: a way of thinking I have grown to love and have begun to apply in my daily life. I choose my words more carefully and notice more when others fail to do the same. Complicated issues have become clearer, and I am much less likely to accept arguments for one side or the other at face value. I notice the assumptions behind statements people make. I see the holes in their logic.

The law seems to be the right crucible for all of my interests. The profession allows for cross-pollination with other disciplines. It combines both the purity of logic and the messiness of humanity. A law degree will help unlock such doors as that of the American consulate's Christmas party and will qualify me to work on an endless supply of problems and puzzles whose answers are of greater importance than those on an LSAT. I will be a part of a community of people who take an active pleasure in understanding how the world works, who engage with it and wrestle with its imperfections. I will be able to continue to use all of the talents that I have refined in my training as a musician—creativity, passion, discipline and humility—and add to them a livelier use of my mind and an interest in a far wider world.

Jamie Lynn Bartholomew

Jamie believes that her strengths as a law school candi-date were her high GPA from a top university, her many extracurricular activities, and her work experience. (She was on the board of directors of a bank.) She thinks her LSAT score was what kept her from being accepted to all of the schools that waitlisted her. She also thinks that applying to law school directly out of undergrad hurt her.

Stats:

LSAT: 162

GPA: 3.9

College attended: Princeton University

Class: 2002

Hometown: West Chester, PA

Gender: Female

Race: White

Law school attending: To be determined. Jamie is re-taking the LSAT and reapplying to law schools next year. She is spending the intervening year studying for a master's degree at Oxford University in England.

Class: 2006

Applied to the following law schools:

Accepted: Georgetown, University of Chicago, University of Virginia

Denied: NYU

Other: Columbia, Harvard, Yale (placed on waitlist by all)

Personal statement:

"Please present yourself, your background and experiences, and your ideas as you wish in a brief personal statement."

Guts

"Power Ten, on this one!" my coxswain roared. Brown was gaining water on us. Quickly. If we did not pick up the pace immediately, we would lose the race. As I pulled harder and harder, harder than I have ever pulled in my entire life, every muscle in my body screamed in protest. My already frantic breathing turned into desperate gasps for air. Sweat poured off my forehead, dripped quickly through my tiger-striped bandanna and into my eyes, leaving my vision a blurry haze of light and darkness. Knowing that the seven other girls in my boat were selflessly pushing through pain just as excruciating as my own, though, enabled me to ignore this overwhelming physical anguish and focus my complete attention on the commands of the coxswain. A few strokes later, the race was over - we were NCAA National Women's Varsity Lightweight Crew Champions!

I had never rowed crew before arriving at Princeton University, so to be able to make the first boat and compete against recruits who had been rowing for years meant that I had a lot of catching up to do. To make up for my lack of experience, I devoted almost all of my free time to training on my own. Whereas my friends passed their Saturday nights socializing and dancing, I spent mine alone at the boathouse, working to improve my stroke. The intense training paid off, though, and by the end of the year I stroked the varsity boat and had the fastest ergometer score on the team.

My dedication to rowing did not go unnoticed by my teammates: before racing season in the spring, I was unanimously elected as a team captain. I was a role model for the other rowers, leading the team by example. Because I was a freshman, a walk-on, no less, and trained harder than any other rower in the boathouse, I set extremely high standards for the rest of my team. The other girls knew that they, too, would had to put their hearts and souls into crew to make the varsity boat and, even more importantly, to earn the respect and support of the team.

Because crew is a sport in which the best rowers do not stand out, a crew boat is only as successful as its ability to work together. Yes, my individual dedication to the sport inspired the other girls, but their devotion to crew equally inspired me. Our team became fiercely committed to each other - this commitment is really what really clenched our victories during racing season. Never in my life have I felt so close to a group of people. So many times I would have stopped, quit, given up even on myself, but did not because I knew that I could not let down the team. Our unwavering support for each other enabled every single one of us to put forth 110% effort every day of the year, at both two-hour practices each day. Without my teammate's encouragement, I never could have handled the grueling "aerobic threshold" practices that literally left me crawling up the steps to the locker room afterwards. I never would have returned to the boathouse after vomiting and then passing out during ergometer tests. And I also never would have been part of a team that won a NCAA National Championship.

The more that I do in the context of a "team", the more I realize that achievement on personal level is just not enough for me. I am still proud of the individual accomplishments in my life, but only in light of how they help the "team," whether it be the varsity lightweight women rowers, the learning-disabled elementary school children that I tutor, the Princeton freshman that I lead on week-long backpacking trips, or the prisoners to whom I teach decision-making skills.

As a Princeton rower, therefore, I leave with more than just a diploma. I face the world with relentless drive, unwavering persistence, and rock solid, invincible guts. Guts to constantly demand more of myself. Guts to perform and work well with others not only on Lake Carnegie, but also in my politics seminar presentation group, in the boardroom at the National Bank of Malvern, or in any other group in which I may find myself. Guts to accept that being the member of a team means everything that I do affects everybody else. Gut to push myself for my teammates even when I would not push myself for myself. I leave Princeton with the experiences of competition, ambition, and most importantly teamwork, that will I will carry with me for the rest of my life.

APPENDIX:
LSAT ANALYTICAL
REASONING

You already know how important your LSAT score will be to your law school application. And if you've taken a practice LSAT, you already have an idea that it's unlike any standardized test you've taken before. For most who take the LSAT, this impression is due primarily to the Analytical Reasoning section—the section we at The Princeton Review call Games, for reasons we'll explain in a moment.

Of the 101 questions in the five sections of the LSAT that count toward your score, either 23 or 24 will come from the Games section. Each LSAT has one Games section, two Logical Reasoning sections—we call the problems that appear in these sections Arguments—and one Reading Comprehension section. (And the fifth section, you ask? That's the experimental section, which can be Games, Arguments, or Reading Comprehension. Basically, the Law School Admissions Council, the people who make the test, are using you as a guinea pig to test the difficulty of questions that will appear on future LSATs.) Each of the Games sections is made up of four separate games—artificial tasks that must be performed in accordance with a set of rules or conditions. Each game is accompanied by five, six, or seven questions, and some games are decidedly more difficult than others. Even the less difficult games, however, can be intimidating to the unprepared test-taker, and most people with substantial LSAT experience still consider this to be the test's most challenging section.

The purpose of this Appendix then, is to provide an introduction to the fundamentals of The Princeton Review's method for approaching games. Although a full treatment of the nuances and variations of this section of the test is beyond the scope of this book, the strategies described here will provide you with a good framework within which to begin your own preparation. For more information on these topics and others of importance to your LSAT score, you should consult our publication *Cracking the LSAT*. Visit our website (www.PrincetonReview.com) for further information about our intensive course and tutoring offerings and for valuable updates and tips about the entire law school application process.

WHY "GAMES"?

Believe it or not, some people actually find these questions fun, but that isn't the only reason we call them games. Here's an extremely simplified example to help demonstrate what they're like.

> People A, B, C, and D, and only those people, are waiting in line at a cash register, not necessarily in that order.

> Person A is somewhere in front of person B in line.

> No one is waiting in line between persons C and D.

The first portion of a game is what we'll call its setup—the fundamental task or situation around which all of the game's questions will be based. In this case, the setup is that four people are waiting in line in some order. The indented items below the setup are what we'll call clues or rules; these limit the ways in which the task can be performed or the situation can be arranged. In this particular case we have two rules, each of which limits the order in which our four people may be positioned in the cash register line.

Obviously there's nothing we can really do with the setup and clues by themselves. Like all games, this one doesn't *completely* specify the order of people in line through its rules; it only *restricts* the order. That's where the questions come in.

> 18. If C is the second person in line, then which one of the following must be true?

This is an "if" question, a type that's asked frequently in Games sections. It provides a restriction in addition to the original rules and then asks you about only those arrangements that fit all those rules. It's important to know that any restriction supplied as part of an "if" question applies *only* to that question. So when they ask the next one . . .

> 19. Which one of the following CANNOT be true?

. . . we're no longer dealing just with cases where C is second, but with any arrangement that follows the *original* rules. This is the big difference between "if" questions and the second major type, called, surprisingly enough, "which" questions.

Whatever kind of question you're working, the basic approach you'll find yourself using will be the same. One way or another, you'll be looking for a way to *visualize* the information in the question. Although the material in the setup and clues is delivered *verbally*, what it describes is something that is fundamentally *spatial*. A lot of what makes games confusing is that people try to work with the words rather than envisioning—and finding a way to represent that envisioning *on paper*—how the players in a game can move relative to one another, where they can or cannot appear, and how the placement of one affects the placement of others.

In the end, working questions well depends on your ability to see them as board games. Every setup will have two major components: the fixed diagram, which serves as the board within which the pieces can move, and the mobile elements, which are the pieces or players that must be located according to the rules.

In the case of our simple example, the best diagram is a set of numbered columns, first through fourth from left to right. Our people—A, B, C, and D—are the elements we're moving around within that board. The rules, then, tell us that A has to appear before (to the left of) B and that C and D must appear adjacent to each other. Certainly it makes more intuitive sense—and suggests some ways of approaching the game—if we think of C and D not as separate elements, but as the two parts of one big piece, a block, that takes up half of our diagram.

This is ultimately why we call these types of questions games. Each one can be solved with a board (diagram), a set of pieces (elements), and a collection of rules to follow in placing the pieces on the board. It's especially important to think of the elements as being mobile rather than fixed in place, since questions will only seldom allow you to arrive at a single fixed arrangement of elements in the diagram. First and foremost, The Princeton Review's strategy for games involves an efficient, accurate, and intuitive way of representing this information on paper.

TEN CRUCIAL FACTS ABOUT LSAT GAMES

Before we get into the details of our step-by-step method, there are a few things you should know about this section's rules, design, and basic strategy.

1. NO SCRATCH PAPER IS ALLOWED.

Don't ask why; it's just the rule. Every games section is four pages long, and you are not permitted to turn to any other section in your test booklet, scribble on your answer sheet, or vandalize your desk in your efforts to get the right answer. You've got the space at the bottom of the page to work with, and that's it. Enjoy!

2. Very few people finish games sections.

If you've taken a practice LSAT, chances are that you've discovered you're with the majority on this one. Many standardized test sections are in fact designed so that a substantial number of test-takers don't finish them, but LSAT games sections are more intractable than most. Although this may sound discouraging at first, it turns out that, in conjunction with several of the other facts listed here, you can actually turn this one to your advantage if you know how.

3. There is no penalty for random guessing, so always answer every question.

If you took the SAT once upon a time, you probably remember something about a "guessing penalty," a quarter-point deduction from your raw score for every question you got wrong. The LSAT does *not* do this. Your raw score is simply the number of right answers you get, no matter how you get them, so with five minutes left in every LSAT section, make sure you fill in all the remaining bubbles for that section on your answer sheet. You can always change the answer to any question you work before time is called, but this way you're certain that you'll never get caught with blanks. When you guess randomly, it's best to use the same letter all the time—your letter of the day—and no, it doesn't matter which one you choose as long as you use the same one throughout the test.

4. There is no *best* answer; there's a *right* answer.

After you've checked out the Logical Reasoning and Reading Comprehension sections of the LSAT, you'll realize that this is a unique feature of games. No matter how good you get at the rest of the exam, it's not possible to be 100 percent certain that the answer you're looking at is in those sections objectively correct; you'll always be looking for the additional confirmation that the other four answers are not as good. On Games, though, you can be certain; which means that if you evaluate answer choice (B) and are certain it's right, you pick it, forget about the other choices, and move on immediately!

5. Four wrong answers equal one right answer.

In a vein similar to the fact above, it's important to realize that finding four choices you can be certain are wrong is equivalent to finding one you're certain is right. Very often—especially when the choices each contain a large amount of information—the most efficient approach to a question is to seek out the four wrong choices rather than trying to verify a right one. When we look at a few games in detail, we'll have more to say as to when you should use one approach and when you should use the other—that is, looking for the right answer.

6. TIME SPENT ON A QUESTION YOU GET WRONG IS WASTED TIME.

Although you always want to move efficiently and confidently through the questions on every LSAT section, a lot of test-takers let their frustration get the better of them on games and adopt a bad strategy. The primary goal here is not to get a chance to work every question; it's to maximize the number of right answers you're getting. Since certainty is possible on Games questions in a way it's not on the other question types, an additional investment of time on a Games question you've narrowed down to two or three choices is *not* a waste—just the opposite, in fact. Guessing when you're down to two means you're giving away (on average) half the time you spent getting that far on the question! Your main goal on this section is to make sure that you turn time into points, and if you cut and run before you've gotten the answer on a Games question, you're wasting time, not saving it.

7. "SURFING" GAMES IS AN ENORMOUS WASTE OF TIME.

As we just said, abandoning a question before you get to the answer is actually giving away time; starting a game without attempting all of its questions is even worse. Whether or not you can expect to finish a Games section, it is a terrible mistake to start one game and then go to another one when the first begins to give you trouble. There's a huge benefit to familiarity with a given game, and most of them are going to seem hard at first. Skipping around just slows the process of gaining familiarity with an individual game, increases nervousness by making the section feel disjointed, and wastes time just in the act of turning pages and looking around. It's fine to read a game and decide at that point that it should be avoided, but once you've begun digging into its questions, you need to press on until you've made a good effort at all of them.

8. The order of the games is not chosen to your advantage.

There are very few things that "never" happen on the LSAT, but here's one: The games are never strictly in increasing order of difficulty. Most often the worst game is the second or third of the section, but even if it's last, the chances are that you'll benefit from scouting the entire section before you dive into any one game. It takes time, practice, and knowledge of game construction to become adept at estimating a given game's difficulty, but even beginners can follow a few simple rules: (1) if you don't know how to diagram a game, avoid it; (2) if it contains several ugly-looking clues, avoid it; and (3) it is rare that the game with the most questions is the easiest on a section, so be sure you know what you're getting into before you attempt a seven-question game.

9. Just do something.

No matter how much you practice, you will always come across some games that confuse you at times. When this happens, the natural impulse is to sit back and take stock; reread the setup or clues, check out your prior work, and thrash around in search of inspiration. A certain amount of this is inevitable when you face a roadblock, but don't let that impulse get the better of you. The way you learn how a game works is to *work with* it, not stare at it. If you can eliminate one answer choice or even just generate one example, you'll be making progress toward getting a feel for the game, understanding how it works, and feeling confident about it. The LSAT is a test of mental toughness; don't let momentary confusion stop you from moving forward.

10. Stay calm and don't rush.

This is the single best piece of advice for working a Games section under timed conditions. If you keep the previous nine facts in mind, you'll work steadily, confidently, and inevitably through the questions in a game. Don't dawdle, but don't give in to the temptation to throw up your hands or search desperately for something to bail you out. You'll do your best on games when you're methodical, collected, and thinking clearly. Don't let the clock drive you to panic.

GAMES PLAN

Now that we have all the groundwork out of the way, it's time to talk about the method for approaching these beasts. As it turns out, a single four-step process is suitable for all the games you'll encounter, although the particular of what you'll be doing in each step will depend in some measure on the particular game in front of you. As you read through the steps, they may seem time-consuming, but with practice they will become second nature. More important, this systematic method will increase your efficiency by making sure that you address all the basic features of the game before you reach the questions, rather than trying to work it all out on the fly. The alternative ad hoc approach most often leads to confusion, nervousness, and serious errors that cost time and points.

You'll notice as you read that each of these steps contains a lot of detail—likely more than you're prepared to absorb as you go through on a first reading. These brief treatments contain several principles that are helpful in some of the thornier or stranger LSAT games that have historically appeared, and as you continue your preparation by working real past LSAT games, you will likely find answers to some of the difficulties you encounter secreted away in a sentence you didn't fully understand the first time you read it. Come back to these descriptions often in your preparation, and hopefully you'll continue to find nuggets that help you refine your approach to, and understanding of, our method for working LSAT games.

STEP 1: SET UP THE GAME

Your goal here is to decide what part of the game serves as the core of its diagram and what part will be its elements; you'll also want to get a basic sense of the bookkeeping rules for the game. We'll address these two concerns separately.

As we said earlier, the idea with games is to try to translate their information into something visual you can work with on the page in the limited space you have. Deciding what will be your game board is the most important concern, and you should let the nature of the game's central task determine what diagram you use. Seen broadly, the central tasks of games can be boiled down to four categories: ordering the elements, grouping the elements, putting the elements into a spatial arrangement, or putting the elements into some other organizational arrangement.

The first two tasks—ordering and grouping—will start off seeming the most natural and easiest for you, and as it turns out, they can be diagrammed similarly.

In both cases, we'll make a *table* as our diagram, with the core of the game situated (most often) across the top of the table in a line. Each row below our header will be dedicated to a single example—an arrangement of elements that conforms to the rules of the game.

In an ordering game, deciding what will be the core of your diagram—the header row of the table—is relatively simple. If a game contains something with a natural order or if the rules use some sort of comparison, then the basis of that comparison provides the core of the diagram. For instance, if the game involves scheduling seven appointments to take place one at a time throughout one day, then the basis of comparison (earlier/later) suggests that the times need to be the core of its diagram—appointments one through seven across the top. Similarly, if five tennis players are being ranked on a ladder, then the basis of comparison (higher/lower) suggests that the ranks need to be the core of the diagram. Games with similar diagrams will result from any basis of comparison that goes in two directions: east/ west, nearer/farther, more/less, and so on.

Grouping games can be a little trickier to identify and set up. Very often they involve things that evidently are groups—assigning employees to committees, seating partygoers at tables, placing children in cars for a carpool—but sometimes they can be more abstract: deciding which of several cities each of four different travelers will visit, which articles of clothing each of three mannequins will display, or on which two days seven various errands will be run. A key difference to note that can help you identify grouping games is that elements can be said to be either *together* or *apart,* and very often the clues will relate elements that must be in the same group or can't be. Most ordering games *don't* include any clues like these.

Once you've identified a grouping game, deciding on the core of its diagram is frequently a simple matter: whatever you have less of should be the header of your table. For instance, using some of the examples cited above, you'll have nine employees and three committees, so the committees should be the core of your diagram, or you'll have four travelers and seven cities, so the travelers should be the core of your diagram. This easy rule of thumb won't unerringly lead you to a diagram every time, but there are relatively few exceptions. If all else fails, remember that a game's clues *most often relate elements to other elements,* not groups to groups.

Once you've decided on a diagram for an ordering or grouping game, place the header of your table near the top of the largest chunk of white space you can find on the page, and then near (preferably above) the header, list the elements you have to work with in an inventory. Having your inventory near your diagram will help you get ideas quickly when you've reached a stopping point in a question you're working.

Not all games fall nicely into the categories of ordering or grouping. Some, for example, will ask you to arrange elements in physical space by placing them in a grid. As you can imagine, a table isn't suitable for diagramming these spatial arrangement games. There are other, more difficult kinds of games that may also call for slightly different types of diagrams. Games that ask you to track information of several different kinds about each slot, games that require you to both group and order elements, and games that give you rules for switching elements' places over time are just a few examples of ones that depend on an organizational arrangement. These most often can't be diagrammed with simple tables either, and call instead for diagrams similar to those you'll use for spatial arrangement games. Later on, once you've gotten examples of the basic types under your belt, we'll show how you have to adjust your approach when you encounter these variants. For now, it's enough to know that although a very large number of LSAT games can be diagrammed using a simple table, not all of them can.

The last thing you need to do before moving on from the first step is to check your basic bookkeeping assumptions. Most of us begin with the assumption that every element is used exactly once—no repeats are permitted, and no element may be left out of your diagram. Although it's true that by far the majority of games are indeed one-to-one, not all of them are. As you continue your practice, you'll encounter games where elements may be used more than once, where not all of them are necessarily used, and even where the number of uses of each element is itself governed by clues. Making an unwarranted assumption about the bookkeeping realities of a game can be disastrous, and in typical lawyerly fashion the test writers will provide language that lets you know, however obliquely, what assumptions you are permitted to make.

Step 2: Symbolize the Clues

The goal of this step is to render the game's clues in a way that allows you to dispense with the test-writers' often convoluted language and instead use a representation of the clue that is clear, complete, and consistent. We'll elaborate on these requirements one at a time.

A clear symbol is one that is visual rather than textual, so instead of reading the clue, you *see* what it means. Although this is an ideal to which sometimes even the best possible symbol can only aspire, it should be the first thing you have in mind as you symbolize a clue. As they begin to practice symbolizing, many test-takers resort naturally to algebraic representations, so that the clue

V's appointment is exactly one hour later than W's

becomes, unfortunately,

$$V = W + 1$$

This is no improvement at all, however, and is not a clear symbol. Certainly it can be understood, but so can the initial language of the clue; the point isn't that the clue be comprehensible but that it be clear. Here's a better representation of the clue.

$$\boxed{\text{W V}}$$

In this symbol we *see* what V and W's relationship would be to each other in a game where appointments are one hour long and take place one at a time. For one thing, the earlier appointment (W's) is on the left, where the earlier appointments should be in our diagram; for another thing, we employ the very simple notation of a block (the rectangle around our elements), which visually and intuitively locks the two elements in place. They must be next to each other in exactly this order. The symbol sums up that information in a way that is accessible at a glance.

In addition to being easily readable, the clue must not cut any corners or foreclose possibilities left open by the clue. That is, the symbol must be complete. Our initial, simplified game about the people standing in line for a cash register provides a useful example.

No one is waiting in line between persons C and D.

Although this is clearly a block, it isn't sufficient to represent it in exactly the same way as we did the one above. Do you see the key difference? Here, there's no implied order of C and D. Some might lazily symbolize it the same way, relying on their memory to supply the information missing from their symbol, but as you'll discover in working games under timed conditions, your mind will have plenty to do without relying on itself to keep track of little technicalities like this one. It's easy enough to add an "or" and write the other possible block, and certainly this is an acceptable choice. Another is to have a separate, intuitive symbol to show when a block is flippable. Here's a common one: the smiley face.

Whichever way you choose, the most important considerations are that your symbol not be any more restrictive than the clue itself and that you not rely more than you have to on your memory in interpreting a symbol.

Finally, as much as possible your symbols should be consistent in several senses. Although it's a part of the discussion above of clarity, it's worth mentioning here that your symbol needs to be consistent with your diagram. If earlier appointments are to the left and later ones to the right, then the clue

> X's appointment is at some time after Y's

should become

> Y—X

because this is the order in which the elements will appear when they're plugged correctly in to the diagram. The dash we've put between them, sometimes called a rubber band, is a symbol we'll use to indicate that the relationship is not fixed and that Y and X may be immediately next to each other, or at opposite ends of the diagram, or at any range in between. It's better than greater-than or less-than signs because you *see* the relationship in a way that's consistent with your diagram.

The fact that we use particular notations to correspond with particular kinds of clues is another facet of consistency, and one you should pay attention to whether you choose to adopt our symbol system or dream up one of your own. Whatever system you use, it needs through habit to become instinctive so that you're not puzzling over your symbol. If you often find yourself going back to read a clue rather than using your symbol for it, then the symbol you've made is not a good one.

There are a few cases, however, in which there is for all practical purposes no such thing as a good symbol for a clue. In those cases, it's still best to make your own version—a paraphrase, hopefully five words or less, of what the clue boils down to. As long as you put it in the list with your other symbols, you won't make the common mistake of forgetting a difficult clue.

Sometimes test-takers who've practiced a good deal can get caught up, especially with difficult clues, in the question of whether their symbols are "right." Don't waste precious testing time wondering whether someone else would symbolize a given clue some other way. The ideal here is to be clear, complete, and consistent, but in the final analysis, as long as your symbol leads you to use the clue correctly, it's the right one.

STEP 3: DOUBLE-CHECK AND MAKE DEDUCTIONS

Before moving on, it's imperative to make certain that you've symbolized all the clues and that the symbols you've chosen are correct. The best way to double-check is to go against the grain; look at your symbol, summarize for yourself what that symbol means, then go back to the text version and verify that your interpretation of the symbol's meaning matches the clue you've been given. Once you've verified a given symbol, make a written check mark beside the clue in the original games text. Then, once you've verified all your symbols, make a quick check through the text to be certain you haven't missed any clues. Under time pressure, missing a clue is one of the most common—and most avoidable—errors that test-takers make.

The reason we do this is clear: since your objective in symbolizing the clues in the first place is to get away from their text renditions, you need to be absolutely certain that your symbols accurately reflect the clues. This means in particular not making pseudo-deductions: assumptions about the meaning of a clue that turn out to be unwarranted. The entire process of double-checking should take only a handful of seconds, and it's time well spent. There's nothing worse than getting halfway through a game and then finding a question that has no correct answer—the usual sign that you've misunderstood a clue along the way.

Once you're sure your symbols are right, you can move on to the heart of this step, making deductions. A deduction is a fact about the game that must be true given all the clues, even though that fact isn't directly stated. This preparatory step for working a game is certainly important, but it's just as important that you not obsess about it or spend too much time looking for deductions that aren't there. Here's a quick list of the places you should always look for deductions.

One-clue automatic deductions: In a game where you're ordering seven elements, the range clue Y—X comes with a built-in deduction. Since Y must have at least one element after it in the order, it can't possibly appear last; similarly, since

X must have at least one element before it, it can't appear first. It's also often profitable to see whether the number of places a block can fit into your diagram is limited just because of the block's sheer size. When we introduce conditional clues in a later sample game, we'll see that they too come with automatic deductions. You'll have to look in different places with different types of clues, but the basic idea here is to examine each clue individually and look at how that clue is going to wind up being reflected in your diagram. These deductions are simple but can be quite helpful.

Two-clue deductions on repeated elements/slots: It's often the case in games that a particular element or a particular area of the diagram is mentioned in two clues. When this happens, there's always a chance that you can combine those two pieces of information to arrive at a deduction. This situation may present you with an opportunity to combine clues and make new automatic deductions, or it may allow you to arrive at a new and quite specific piece of information about the clue or slot, but the point is that you should always attempt to combine information when the opportunity presents itself. There won't always be a deduction to find, but these are prime signals of them.

Deductions on ground rules: A ground rule is a very special kind of clue you'll find in some games, one that applies to a large number of your elements or to a large portion of your diagram. For example, if you're arranging books of poetry and fiction in a line on a shelf, and one clue tells you that books of poetry cannot be beside one another, then this clue to applies to all of the books of poetry and is likely to yield fruitful deductions, especially if another clue gives you the definite location of a book. When they're present, ground rules like this one are powerful clues and should always be examined when you're looking for deductions.

Lather, rinse, repeat: Realize that any deduction you make in turn functions like a new clue, and often that fact itself, or in conjunction with other clues, can lead to further deductions.

There are a few cautions you should keep in mind when you're making deductions. First, understand that deductions are definite things—facts that are true all the time. A deduction does not begin with language like "If this element is here, then we also know . . . ." This kind of thinking will be important in some questions, but now is not the time for it. You should not be generating random examples as part of step 3 or looking into specific cases.

Second, don't confuse deductions with suspicions. Some test-takers rashly accept as deductions things they're "pretty sure" are true all the time. If some leap of intuition leads you to suspect that something must be true all the time, verify it for certain before you write it down as a deduction. Pseudo-deductions can be disastrous on LSAT games.

Third, realize that not all games have significant deductions, and not all deductions are findable at this stage in working a game. This is where experience and a solid process come in. Look for deductions in the places mentioned above—the more games you work as part of your preparation, the better you'll get at knowing where to look—and once you're done, you're done. You will certainly encounter games where there are deductions that you don't find at this stage; there are occasionally hidden deductions that you have to try several examples to find. The point of this step isn't to waste your time or make you doubt yourself; it's to give you as much information as possible going into your first question. Having deductions in hand will make your overall approach to the game faster and more efficient by saving you time on questions, but only as long as you don't dawdle here. Find what you can, then move on. Remember that no game has ever worked itself by being stared at intensely.

Finally, realize that the search for deductions doesn't end here. As you work through the questions on a game, you will occasionally come across other deductions that you didn't notice at first. As mentioned above, it's important not to take a mere suspicion and turn it into a deduction, but as you get to know a game by working questions, you may realize that there's something that's happening all the time, and a little bit of investigation can tell you why. When you find a deduction like this, be sure to use it in subsequent questions.

STEP 4: ATTACK THE QUESTIONS IN A GOOD ORDER

Once you have a diagram, useful and correct representations of the clues, and a solid sense of anything else that must be true all the time, you're ready to rip through the questions. Like the games section itself, however, the questions within a game are put in a particular order for a reason, and it isn't often chosen to your advantage.

There are two major types of games questions: "if" questions and "which" questions. Although you can most often tell what type a question is just by looking at its first word, it isn't always that simple. The essential difference is that an "if" question will add information to the clues of a game, whereas a "which" question adds nothing and asks you to deal with the game just as it is.

What kind would you rather work first? Since "if" questions provide you with a starting point—an initial piece of information that you can often plug in to your diagram and then deduce other things from—these are the best questions to start with. "If" questions are specific; they provide a good way of gaining familiarity with a game; and as an additional bonus, you'll find that some of the work you do on "if" questions can be reused as evidence when you're working on "which" questions.

"Which" questions, as mentioned before, provide no additional information. Although it's sometimes the case that a "which" question asks about a deduction you made in step 3, it's just as often true that you have to use process of elimination on the answer choices individually to find the right one. Working answer choices is time-consuming and can be quite confusing. You want as much experience with the game as you can get before you tackle these.

Clearly not all "if" questions are easy, just as not all "which" questions are diabolically difficult. This is why the title of this step urges you to work the questions in a *good* order. If you start the first "if" question and discover that you're really struggling, it's perfectly all right to move on to the next "if" question and come back. In rare cases, you may find yourself preferring to work some or all of the "which" questions before you come back to a particularly dastardly "if." But the place to start—the basic method you should use when you come at first to any game—is to attack the "if" questions first, then move on to the others. This will increase both your accuracy and your efficiency.

Although it's easy to identify the "if"/"which" difference and characterize these questions in general, you'll find that there are other things about the questions that you need to register in answering them. A question may ask what "must be true," what "could be true," or variations on these—"must be false," "could be false," "could be true EXCEPT," and so forth. Some questions will ask for lists of where an element could go or which elements could fill a certain slot in your diagram; others will ask you to count possible arrangements or identify impossible ones. Different questions require slightly different strategies and different approaches to the answer choices, so it's mostly by example and practice that you'll learn what you most need to know to really refine your approach to LSAT games.

TRYING IT OUT

The bulk of this treatment consists of three sample games, chosen to illustrate three basic types of tasks that you'll encounter. As you move through the next few sections, you'll want to have a pencil handy. This is your chance to begin practicing the step-by-step process we've outlined for you and get a sense of how it works in realistic situations.

The basic format of each of the following sections is the same; we'll introduce each example by going through some of the new skills and information required for that game. We encourage you to read these introductions first, since otherwise you may struggle with diagrams or clues that are unfamiliar to you.

Once you've read the introduction, it's time for you to tackle the game. Although you may want to keep track of how long it takes you, speed isn't your main concern here. In these early examples you should focus on following the step-by-step approach, noting similarities and differences, and trying out the new concepts you've learned.

Only when you've done your best with a given game's questions should you move on. You'll find the credited responses listed immediately after the game, along with full explanations of why those responses are right and how you should have arrived at them. Although you will find some of the questions difficult, these games have not been chosen primarily to stump you; even if you got every question in a game right, you should still examine the explanations to find tips on how to approach the questions most efficiently. You may discover that you could have answered some of them by doing far less work!

SAMPLE GAME ONE: ORDERING

This first illustration is an example of a game based around an ordering task—in this case, scheduling the display of seven artists' work over the course of seven weeks in an art gallery. If you've read all the text thus far, you should already be familiar with most of what's required to work this game successfully. Here are a few brief tips on things that might be unfamiliar.

SYMBOLIZING ANTIBLOCKS

The game includes one clue that describes two elements that *can't* be next to each other. Although we've seen blocks before—pairs of elements that must appear together—we haven't yet mentioned this particular type of clue. As you might expect, since the clues are pretty closely related, the symbol for an antiblock is closely related, too.

A cannot appear immediately before B

becomes

|A·B|

COMPOSITE RANGE CLUES

We've already seen range clues: if Y has to appear before X, then we symbolize it as Y—X. But this game includes one clue that describes an element that has to appear before *two* others. Although it's of course possible to symbolize this as two separate range clues, we'd like to represent the information as compactly as possible—namely, in one symbol. As it turns out, this isn't too difficult.

C must appear before both D and E

becomes

It's very important to note that this symbol, like its clue, implies no particular relationship between D and E; you can think of them as being at the ends of separate branches of a tree, and either branch may be longer than the other. Like all range clues, this one doesn't tell us how close D and E are to C, just that they both need to appear to the right.

COMBINING CLUES IN DEDUCTIONS

As mentioned above, it's advantageous to put as much information as possible into one symbol. This doesn't just work for symbolizing a composite range clue; it also applies to cases in ordering games where range clues can be combined with one another or even with blocks. This game provides an opportunity to do this during your deduction step, and combining clues can be quite helpful in making further deductions. Take a look at this set of three simple clues, assuming that they belong to a one-to-one ordering game with seven elements.

(1) A must appear immediately before B.

(2) A must appear before C.

(3) B must appear before D.

Although we could symbolize all three separately, what automatic deductions would we make out of them by themselves?

(1) A isn't seventh; B isn't first.

(2) A isn't seventh; C isn't first.

(3) B isn't seventh; D isn't first.

In sum:

A isn't seventh, B isn't first or seventh,

C isn't first, and D isn't first.

Now take a look at this combined symbol of the set of clues. We've arrived at this simply by cobbling the symbols together around their repeated elements.

This gives us a much more complete sense of what's going on. Just by counting the number of elements that have to go before or after those in our diagram, we arrive at this set of deductions:

> A isn't seventh, sixth, or fifth.
>
> B isn't first, seventh, or sixth.
>
> C isn't first or second.
>
> D isn't first or second.

Combining clues where possible in an ordering game can produce quite a lot of information quickly, since bigger clues are more difficult to fit into a diagram.

Now try the game on the next page. Good luck!

Over a span of seven consecutive weeks, an art gallery will feature the work of seven young artists—J, K, L, M, P, Q, and S. Each week exactly one of these artists' works will be featured, and each artist's work will be featured for exactly one week. The order in which the artists' works are featured is subject to the following constraints:

K's work will not be featured in the sixth week.

M's work and K's work will not be featured in consecutive weeks.

L's work will be featured in a later week than the week in which Q's work is featured.

J's work will be featured in the week either immediately before or immediately after the week in which P's work is featured.

Both M's work and K's work will be featured in later weeks than the week in which J's work is featured.

1. Which one of the following CANNOT be true?

    (A) L's work is featured during the
         second week.

    (B) L's work is featured during the
         third week.

    (C) M's work is featured during the
         third week.

    (D) Q's work is featured during the
         sixth week.

    (E) S's work is featured during the
         fifth week.

2. If P's work is featured during the fourth week, then which one of the following could be true?

    (A) J's work is featured during the
         fifth week.

    (B) M's work is featured during the
         sixth week.

(C)   Q's work is featured during the
       sixth week.

(D)   S's work is featured during the
       first week.

(E)   S's work is featured during the
       third week.

3.   If S's work is featured during the third week, then which one of the
     following must be false?

(A)   K's work is featured during the
       fourth week.

(B)   M's work is featured during the
       seventh week.

(C)   P's work is featured during the
       second week.

(D)   Q's work is featured during the
       fifth week.

(E)   Q's work is featured during the
       sixth week.

4.   Which one of the following could be true?

(A)   J's work is featured during the
       fourth week, and Q's work is
       featured during the sixth week.

(B)   L's work is featured during the
       second week, and M's work is
       featured during the sixth week.

(C)   M's work is featured during the
       fourth week, and S's work is
       featured during the second
       week.

(D) M's work is featured during the fifth week, and Q's work is featured during the sixth week.

(E) S's work is featured during the second week, and Q's work is featured during the fifth week.

5. If S's work is featured during the fourth week, then which one of the following is a complete and accurate list of weeks during which L's work could be featured?

(A) sixth

(B) third, seventh

(C) sixth, seventh

(D) fifth, sixth, seventh

(E) third, fifth, sixth, seventh

6. If L's work is featured during the fourth week, then which one of the following must be true?

(A) J's work is featured during an earlier week than the week during which S's work is featured.

(B) L's work is featured during an earlier week than the week during which P's work is featured.

(C) M's work is featured during an earlier week than the week during which L's work is featured.

(D) M's work is featured during an earlier week than the week during which S's work is featured.

(E) Q's work is featured during an earlier week than the week during which J's work is featured.

ANSWERS

1. (B)

2. (D)

3. (E)

4. (D)

5. (C)

6. (A)

EXPLANATIONS

Set Up

We'll use a conventional table for this game, numbered with weeks 1 through 7 across the top. Make sure to include an inventory of the elements involved.

J K L M P Q S

Symbolize

Clue 1:

This is a clue that can be symbolized directly in your diagram. Whenever you work a game, it's a good idea to reserve the top row to represent clues like this one and any subsequent deductions you may make.

Clue 2:

Clue 3:   Q—L

Clue 4:

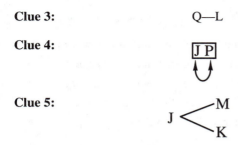

Clue 5:

Always double-check your clues.

Deduce

The big deduction here results from combining clues 4 and 5 around their repeated element, J. The result is this combined symbol:

We're actually not done yet. As you almost certainly noticed when you worked the game, the two elements that have to come after our JP block are also those mentioned in the antiblock in clue 2! Although it's difficult to combine these two facts in a symbol, you can see that there is something more to be deduced here. Ordinarily, a symbol like the combined one above would have to be spread over, at minimum, four spots—one for each of the elements in the symbol. But now, since M and K can't go next to each other, we're forced to put at least one additional spot between them. Thus, even though we can't really represent it in a new symbol, we can tell that there's no way our JP block could occupy slots 4 and 5, or any pair later than that. That leaves us with 1-2, 2-3, or 3-4 as the only possible positions for our JP block, and although we don't want to get into individual cases, we should at least indicate this narrowed set of possibilities at the top of our diagram. With a flippable block this can be a little unwieldy to draw, but you should find a way of representing it that you understand.

Don't forget the automatic deductions from our range clues, either. Clue 3 guarantees us that Q isn't last and L isn't first. Similarly, our combined clue tells us that neither M nor K can be first or second. The result is a diagram that looks like this:

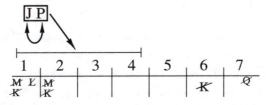

With this material in hand, you're ready to work the questions.

1. **Which CANNOT be true?** This should be a question you work after you've tried all the "if" questions. On a question like this one, you have to go directly to the answer choices. There's a chance that the answer will be an initial deduction you made, but more likely you'll have to work the choices one at a time. Remember: Once you've found the right answer, you're done!

   (A) Try it, and you'll find this is possible. Here's one way it could be done:

1	2	3	4	5	6	7
Q	L	P	J	K	S	M

   (B) **This is the credited response.** L third means that Q must appear earlier—either first or second. That leaves fourth and fifth as the earliest pair of open spots for our JP block, but according to our deductions this is impossible. Trying it would force us to put M and K next to each other in sixth and seventh, which breaks the game's second rule.

   (C) For your reference, here's an example where this can be true:

1	2	3	4	5	6	7
J	P	M	Q	S	L	K

   (D) For your reference, here's an example where this can be true:

1	2	3	4	5	6	7
P	J	K	S	M	Q	L

   (E) See the example in (C) for a case where this can be true.

2. **If P is fourth, which could be true?** The key on questions like these is to deduce everything you can before going to the answer choices. P fourth means that J is third by our deductions; J fifth would force M and K to appear next to each other.

   So J is third, and M and K must be fifth and seventh, although we can't be sure which is in which slot. At this point, all we have left is our Q—L range clue and S. There are more than two arrangements possible from here, so it'd be a waste of time to diagram all of them. We can, however, tell that Q can't possibly be sixth—the last open spot—and as always, L can't be first. Here's the diagram we wind up with:

$$\underset{Ł}{1} \mid 2 \mid \underset{J}{3} \mid \underset{P}{4} \mid \underset{M/K}{5} \mid \overset{Q}{6} \mid \underset{K/M}{7}$$

With this information in hand, you can quickly scan and see that the only choice that could be true is **(D), the credited response**.

3. **If S is third, which must be false?** As always on an "if" question, we deduce first. The first question is where our JP block goes, and it's relatively easy to see that it can't possibly go after S. So the block is in first and second, and beyond that we have many different possibilities. We know Q can't be seventh and K can't be sixth—these are always true—but then L can't be fourth, which is the earliest open spot remaining. Here's the diagram of what we know:

$$\underset{J/P}{1} \mid \underset{P/J}{2} \mid \underset{S}{3} \mid \overset{Ł}{4} \mid 5 \mid \overset{K}{6} \mid \overset{Q}{7}$$

The question here is what must be false—in other words, what can't possibly be true. So four of our choices will be possible, and one won't be. Since none of the choices directly contradicts a deduction we've made so far, we'll have to check them out one at a time.

(A) Nothing wrong with this. Here's a quick diagram:

$$\underset{J}{1} \mid \underset{P}{2} \mid \underset{S}{3} \mid \underset{K}{4} \mid \underset{Q}{5} \mid \underset{L}{6} \mid \underset{M}{7}$$

(B) Nothing wrong with this. The example in (A) shows how this could be true.

(C) Nothing wrong with this. The example in (A) shows how this could be true.

(D) Nothing wrong with this. The example in (A) shows how this could be true.

(E) **This is the credited response.** It's the only choice left. If you actually try it, you'll see that it can't work because if Q is sixth, then L has to be seventh. Then our only two spaces left open for M and K are immediately next to each other.

4. **Which one of the following could be true?** This is a question to work after you've done all the "if" questions. Sometimes there are shortcuts on these types of questions, but in this case the choices contain no obvious rule violations, and in all likelihood you haven't generated a previous example where one of the choices is illustrated. (However, if you look at our earlier discussion of question 1, you'll find that the example we provided for choice (D) happens to illustrate the right answer on this one.) Most likely, though, you'll have to move to the answer choices and work them one at a time.

(A) This can't be true. J fourth means P must be third, since trying to put P fifth forces M and K to appear next to each other. But then putting Q sixth forces L to be seventh, which leaves only one space open after the JP block.

(B) This can't be true. L second means Q must be first. M sixth means that K can't appear fifth or seventh, so the latest K could appear is fourth. At this point, there's no space in the diagram big enough to accommodate our JP block.

(C) This can't be true. M fourth means the JP block has to occupy two of the first three spaces. But then putting S second doesn't leave two adjacent spaces open to accommodate the block.

(D) **This is the credited response.** Here's an example showing how this can be done:

1	2	3	4	5	6	7
P	J	K	S	M	Q	L

(E) This can't be true. S second and Q fifth leaves third and fourth as the only pair of spaces where the JP block could possibly appear. But this forces M and K to appear next to each other in the last two spaces, to say nothing of L.

5. **If S is fourth, where could L appear?** You start a question like this one the same way you start any "if" question: deduce what you can. S fourth means that the JP block must occupy two of the first three spaces in your diagram; certainly, then, either J or P is second. We've known from the start that L can't be first, but now since two of the first three spaces are

occupied, we know L can't be third, either—that would leave no space for Q to appear before L.

Once we have that information, it's important to eliminate answer choices that contain it. (B) and (E) both incorrectly claim that L could be third. Evidently L can be sixth, since all the remaining choices contain that space. The only real questions remaining are whether L could be fifth or seventh or both.

Try fifth. L fifth means that Q must appear in the lone remaining open space before L. But then the only spots open for M and K are sixth and seventh, which would violate rule 2. So L can't be fifth; eliminate (D).

Try seventh. It's relatively easy to see that this is possible:

1	2	3	4	5	6	7
P	J	M	S	K	Q	L

That makes **(C) the credited response**.

6. **If L is fourth, which must be true?** L fourth means that the JP block occupies two of the first three spaces. Since Q must appear before L, Q must occupy the remaining open space in the first three. That forces M and K to appear fifth and seventh, not necessarily in that order. The remaining element, S, must be sixth. Here's the diagram:

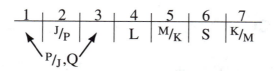

Our diagram represents a lot of possibilities, but the only choice that is true in all of them is **(A), the credited response**.

SAMPLE GAME TWO: GROUPING

Now that we've seen an ordering game and gotten a basic idea of approaches to some "if" and "which" questions, it's time to look at another basic task: grouping. The diagrams for games like these look quite similar to those for ordering games. One big difference is that the headers don't have a "natural order"—groups are just groups, with no one greater than another. The most important difference, however, is that groups usually have multiple elements, so you'll want to create slots within each group to keep track of how many elements go in each place.

This game introduces a few crucial concepts and methods that we haven't seen before. These are all relatively common on LSAT games.

DIFFERENT ELEMENT TYPES

In our previous example, the seven artists were all the same type of element. There was nothing different about J and P other than their names. In this game, however, we have eight elements total, but four of them are of one type and four are of another. When you come across this situation in a game, it's important for your inventory and your work to reflect the difference in element types as clearly as possible. In this case, since there are only two, we should use uppercase/lowercase differences to indicate the difference in type. If there were more than two, we would be forced to use subscripts or shapes to indicate the difference.

COUNTING CLUES

The first clue in this game compares the number of one type of element in a group to the number of that type in another group. Counting clues like this one are seen relatively often in grouping games, and although they are difficult to symbolize visually, they are *extremely* important in working the game. At worst, you should come up with an easy paraphrase of what the clue means and write that down. At best, you'll be able to see that the counting clue results in a very few legal possibilities and you'll use a list of possible scenarios instead of a symbol for the clue. Ask yourself, as you make deductions based on the counting clue, whether there's any way you can characterize the range of possibilities it allows.

CONDITIONAL CLUES

These are very frequently seen on the LSAT and must be handled carefully. Although there are other ways of writing the text of conditional clues, the most common phrasing looks like this:

If [*first thing*], then [*second thing*].

Although in our daily lives we use "if . . . then" statements somewhat loosely, on the LSAT this kind of clue has quite a specific, formal interpretation. This clue tells us nothing more than that whenever the statement [*first thing*] is true, the statement [*second thing*] is also true. The symbol we use for a conditional clue indicates visually that this is a one-sided relationship:

first thing ⟶ *second thing*

We use an arrow because this relationship goes *only* in one direction. In using this symbol, you must never go against the arrow. For instance, imagine a game with three groups and this clue:

If A is in group 1, then B is in group 2.

The symbol here would be

A1 ⟶ B2

It is extremely important to use this symbol properly. In any case where you found out that A was in 1, you would immediately conclude that B is in 2. So far, so good. Suppose, though, that you were working a question where you found out that B is in group 2. What could you conclude?

Nothing. This is the point of using the arrow as the symbol and in thinking of this as a one-sided relationship. When B is in group 2, it's certainly possible that A is in group 1, but it needn't be. A could be in either of groups 2 or 3 as well. If this seems counterintuitive to you, then join the club—that's one of the reasons conditional clues pop up so often on the LSAT. In conversation, we use "if . . . then" statements to mean more than they actually do from the standpoint of formal logic. The thing you have to remember is this: Follow the arrow!

There's only one new thing we can properly conclude from our clue above—the automatic deduction that goes with any conditional clue. It's called the **contrapositive** of the statement. Suppose you're working a question where you find out that B isn't in group 2—maybe it's placed in group 1 or group 3, or the condition on an "if" question tells you simply that it isn't in 2. Now you can conclude something. With B someplace else, you know *for certain* that A can't be in group 1. Why? Because whenever A is in group 1, B has to be in group 2. Since the latter didn't happen in this case, the former can't either.

The contrapositive of a conditional statement is easy to generate once you have a symbol for it; simply change the order of the statements around the arrow, then negate both of them. If we **flip and negate** the conditional symbol above in this way, here's the symbol we wind up with:

$$\cancel{B2} \longrightarrow \cancel{A1}$$

As always, we have to read this by only going *with* the arrow: whenever B isn't in 2, A can't be in 1. This is the *only other thing* that we can conclude from our conditional clue, and it's so important that whenever you see a conditional clue on a game, you should immediately represent its contrapositive—don't wait for deductions to do it.

A quick final quiz about conditionals: Suppose we're working still another question, and we find out that A is not in group 1. What else can we conclude?

That's right, *nothing*. It certainly might be true that B isn't in 2, but there's no requirement either way. Putting B in 2 and A in any other group does not violate either our clue or its contrapositive.

With that in mind, take a stab at this game. And remember that when you're working with symbols for conditional clues, *go with the arrow*.

A bakery is putting eight of its pastries on display: four cakes (angel food, Black Forest, devil's food, and German chocolate) and four pies (key lime, lemon meringue, quince, and sweet potato). In the bakery there are three display areas—the window, along with refrigerated cases numbered one and two. The display in each refrigerated case will include exactly three pastries, at least one cake, and at least one pie; the window display will include two pastries of any type. The display of pastries must conform to the following restrictions:

There cannot be more cakes displayed in refrigerated case number one than are displayed in refrigerated case number two.

The angel food and Black Forest cakes must be included in the same display area.

The key lime and lemon meringue pies cannot be included in the same display area.

The German chocolate cake cannot be displayed in the window, and if it is displayed in refrigerated case number one, then the sweet potato pie must be displayed in refrigerated case number two.

1. Which of the following is an acceptable arrangement of pastries in the bakery's display areas?

(A) window: angel food cake, lemon meringue pie; refrigerated case one: devil's food cake, quince pie, sweet potato pie; refrigerated case two: Black Forest cake, German chocolate cake, key lime pie

(B) window: devil's food cake, quince pie; refrigerated case one: German chocolate cake, key lime pie, lemon meringue pie; refrigerated case two: angel food cake, Black Forest cake, sweet potato pie

(C) window: devil's food cake, sweet potato pie; refrigerated case one: angel food cake, Black Forest cake, key lime pie; refrigerated case two: German chocolate cake, lemon meringue pie, sweet potato pie

(D) window: lemon meringue pie, quince pie; refrigerated case one: devil's food cake, German chocolate cake, key lime pie; refrigerated case two: angel food cake, Black Forest cake, sweet potato pie

(E) window: quince pie, sweet potato pie; refrigerated case one: devil's food cake, German chocolate cake, key lime pie; refrigerated case two: angel food cake, Black Forest cake, lemon meringue pie

2. Which one of the following could be the three pastries displayed together in refrigerated case one?

(A) angel food cake, Black Forest cake, German chocolate cake

(B) devil's food cake, German chocolate cake, quince pie

(C) devil's food cake, quince pie, sweet potato pie

(D) German chocolate cake, key
   lime pie, quince pie

(E) German chocolate cake, key
   lime pie, sweet potato pie

3. If the devil's food and German chocolate cakes are not displayed together,
   then each of the following could be true EXCEPT

(A) the angel food cake is displayed in refrigerated case
   one

(B) the Black Forest cake is displayed in the window

(C) the German chocolate cake
   is displayed in refrigerated
   case one

(D) the key lime pie is displayed
   in the window

(E) the quince pie is displayed in
   refrigerated case two

4. Which one of the following could be the two pastries displayed together
   in the window?

(A) the angel food cake and the
   key lime pie

(B) the devil's food cake and the
   quince pie

(C) the devil's food cake and the
   sweet potato pie

(D) the German chocolate cake
   and the lemon meringue pie

(E) the quince and sweet potato
   pies

5. If the sweet potato pie is displayed in the window, then which one of the following must be true?

(A) the Black Forest cake is displayed in refrigerated case two

(B) the devil's food cake is displayed in refrigerated case two

(C) the key lime pie is displayed in refrigerated case one

(D) the lemon meringue pie in displayed in refrigerated case two

(E) the quince pie is displayed in the window

6. If the Black Forest cake is displayed in the window, then how many different displays of pastries are possible for refrigerated case one?

(A) three

(B) four

(C) five

(D) six

(E) seven

ANSWERS

1. (D)

2. (D)

3. (A)

4. (E)

5. (B)

6. (D)

EXPLANATIONS

Set Up

As we mentioned in the introduction to this game, what we need to do here is make a table with our three groups and make sure our inventory uses capitalization to distinguish between cakes and pies. But there are other items of information relevant to our setup that are related in the initial chunk of text. For one thing, we learn that refrigerated cases one and two each contain three elements, while the window contains only two. We should use blanks in our setup to indicate how many slots there are in each group. Even more important, we learn that cases one and two must each contain at least one cake and at least one pie. We should also include this in our initial diagram—an easy way to deal with this very common type of clue is to reserve the space on the left end of each group for a cake and the space on the right end for a pie. Here's a great way to indicate all this:

C: A B D G
p: k l q s

1	2	w
$\overline{C}$ _ $\overline{p}$	$\overline{C}$ _ $\overline{p}$	_ _

Symbolize

Clue 1: Here's that counting clue we warned you about. Although you may not have thought about it before you got to the deductions, this clue limits the possible assignments of cakes and pies somewhat. For example, whenever there are two cakes in case one, there must also be two cakes in case two, and the rest of the spaces are occupied by pies. On the other hand, if there's only one cake in case one, then there may be either one or two cakes in case two. Although we said earlier that we shouldn't spend precious time making contingent deductions, in this case the clue is difficult to symbolize, and it's relatively easy to list the three basic scenarios that this clue permits.

1	2	w
CCp	CCp	pp
Cpp	CCp	Cp
Cpp	Cpp	CC

Notice that we haven't tried to imagine which cakes and pies can go in which places in each scenario—this really would expend too much time. But with a list of the possible scenarios to refer to, you should be able to work the questions more efficiently; sometimes just one piece of information will tell you for certain which scenario you're working with.

Clue 2: Note that on a grouping game, we don't have to concern ourselves with whether or not a block is flippable, since there's no required order to the slots within a group. This symbol simply means that the two elements have to appear together:

$$\boxed{A\ B}$$

Clue 3:

$$\boxed{k\!\!\!/\,\cancel{l}}$$

Clue 4: This is really two clues rolled into one. The first part guarantees us that G can't go in the window, which we can indicate directly at the top of our diagram. The second part is a conditional clue, which we symbolize along with its contrapositive:

$$G1 \longrightarrow s2$$
$$\cancel{s2} \longrightarrow G2$$

We've done something in writing the contrapositive for which you always need to be on the lookout in a grouping game—this isn't exactly what we get when we flip and negate. The second part of the contrapositive is that G isn't in case one, but putting this fact together with the fact that G can't ever be in the window, we realize that if G isn't in case one, it absolutely has to be in case two. Since **positive representations** like this one are always easier to use than negative symbols, we've gone ahead and written it this way. You should look for opportunities to do this, with the understanding that you must always make certain you've done it correctly when you double-check your clues.

As mentioned, you of course always double-check before moving on.

Deduce

In this case, we've done several things that might be called deductions already. We've written out the possible distributions of cakes and pies, made the contrapositive of our conditional clue, and even paraphrased it—if the sweet potato pie isn't in refrigerated case two, then the German chocolate cake *must* be in case two—to make it more useful. These are all relatively simple applications of the respective clues, and it's perfectly all right to do these kinds of things when you initially symbolize. Always, though, look for further deductions before you move on to the questions.

In this case, there isn't really anything to find. Antiblocks, you'll learn with experience, don't often lead to further deductions, and conditional clues don't usually offer a great deal beyond their contrapositives. We hope you took a close look at that AB block. Although there isn't anything you can deduce for certain from it at this point, it's clearly going to be important in the questions. Not only is it large, but both the elements in the block are cakes; chances are that the placement of this block is going to tell you a lot about which counting scenario you're working with in any given case.

1. **Which is an acceptable arrangement?** Although ordinarily we do "which" questions on a second pass, this is a special—and common—type of "which" question that should be worked first. It asks us to find the choice that conforms to all the rules, and the answer choices are complete listings of where the elements are placed. It's easy, then, to take the rules one at a time and eliminate the choice or choices that violate them. Not all

games have a **grab-a-rule** question like this one, but if they do, it will appear first. And if a game you're working has a grab-a-rule question, you should definitely work it first.

(A) This choice violates rule 2 by having A and B separated.

(B) This choice violates rule 3 by having k and l together.

(C) This choice violates rule 1 by having more cakes in case one than there are in case two.

(D) **This is the credited response.**

(E) This choice violates rule 4 by having G in case one but s not in case two.

2. **Which three pastries could be displayed together in refrigerated case one?** This question is a great illustration of why you should most often work "which" questions on a second pass. Since this is an incomplete listing of the elements' placement—here, we're seeing only the assignment of elements to case one—there will be some answer choices that violate rules in ways that aren't obvious. For instance, choice (A) has three cakes in the same case, which we know can't happen, and choice (E) has G in case one but s also in case one. Since both of these obviously violate rules they should both be eliminated. That leaves us three choices left to work on.

This is where your prior work comes in. Since a "which" question imposes no additional conditions beyond those that apply to the entire game, your work on earlier "if" questions can always be used as a source of evidence and raw material. Thus, before you begin to work on answer choices one at a time in a question like this one, you should scan your past examples on the off chance that you happen to have encountered a question where you generated an example that matches one of the answer choices. In this case you find one: **(D), the credited response**, is one of the arrangements we generated in the course of answering question 6, so no further work is necessary!

For your reference, here are explanations of how the other choices violate this game's rules.

(A) As mentioned above, this puts three cakes in one case.

(B) DGq in case one means that our AB block must go in case two to make the numbers of cakes in each case conform to rule 1. G in case one means that s must be the third element in case two. The two remaining elements—k and l—must go together in the window, which violates rule 3.

(C) Dqs in case one means that G must be in case two (contrapositive of rule 4), so the AB block must go in the window. The last two elements—k and l—must go together in case two, which again violates rule 3.

(D) **This is the credited response.**

(E) As mentioned above, this violates rule 4 with G and s together in case one.

3. **If D and G aren't together, which choice can't be true?** As always, we begin by deducing what we can, but in this case it isn't much. Even if we consider that this breaks down into two initial scenarios—G is displayed in either case one or case two—there are still multiple possibilities for placing D in each scenario. Since we're dealing with a situation where there are more than two scenarios to work through, we're done with making deductions; move to the answer choices immediately. We'll try to make each one true, but don't forget about the condition in the question!

(A) **This is the credited response.** As often happens in questions where we have no choice but to go to the answers, we find the right one quickly. If A is in case one, then B must be also. Then, in order to satisfy the numbering requirements in rule 1, we must put the other two cakes together in case two. But this violates the condition in the question! We're done.

(B) For your reference, here's an example showing that this choice can be true:

1	2	w
G k q	D l s	A B

(C) This can be true, as illustrated in the example in (B).

(D) This can be true. Here's one way it can be done:

1	2	w
G l q	A B s	D k

(E) This can be true. Here's one way it can be done:

1	2	w
D s k	G l q	A B

4. **Which could be together in the window?** Here's another question like question 2. (A) contains a relatively obvious rule violation—A without B—and (D) plainly violates rule 4 with G in the window. Again, though, if you're doing this question on a second pass, you can scan your prior work and avoid the time-consuming need to narrow down from here. Answer choice **(E), the credited response,** is one of the possibilities we encountered in our work for question 5!

Just in case, here's a description of the problems with the other answer choices.

(A) As we said above, this choice includes A in a display without B.

(B) Dq in the window means that the AB block must go in case two, and G must go in case one to follow rule 1. G in one means s must be in two (rule 4). Then the last two elements—k and l—must go together in case one, the only two remaining spaces. But this violates rule 3.

(C) Ds in the window means that the AB block must go in case two, and

G must go in case one to follow rule 1. G in one means s must be in two because of rule 4, but this choice has already placed s in the window.

(D) As we said above, this choice violates rule 4 by putting G in the window.

(E) **This is the credited response.**

5. **If s is in the window, which must be true?** As always on an "if" question, we begin by deducing what we can: if s is not in case two, then G must be in case two, by the contrapositive of rule 4. The only place the AB block will fit is case one, so in order to satisfy clue 1 we have to put the remaining cake, D, in case two with G. What's left to place, then, are k, l, and q; we have to keep k and l separate, but we have one slot open in each of the groups to accommodate them, and q will go in whatever space remains. We can't diagram all of the possibilities, so let's leave it at this:

$$\frac{1}{\text{A B \_}} \quad | \quad \frac{2}{\text{G D \_}} \quad | \quad \frac{\text{w}}{\text{s \_}} \quad \boxed{\text{k}}, \text{q}$$

The only choice that's consistent with our diagram is **(B), the credited response**.

6. **If B is in the window, how many different arrangements can we make for case one?** This is everyone's favorite—a **count-the-ways** question. We start it the same way we start any "if" question: by making all the deductions we can. B in the window means that A must be there, too. Now we have to put one cake in each of the display cases, but there's no particular reason we have to put either cake in either place.

This is where we have to be careful. On a count-the-ways question, you need to find a systematic way of counting without leaving any possibilities out or counting any possibility twice. As often happens with games, the easiest way to do this is to break the possibilities into two overarching scenarios and then work on the scenarios separately, adding together the total possibilities we get from each overarching scenario to get our answer. We've just seen a great way to do this on this question; either D is in one and G is in two, or vice versa. We'll work the scenarios one at a time.

With D in one and G in two, we have to make sure we keep k and l separate. Either can go in either group, so we'll put **placeholders** in our diagram to indicate this fact. There's one slot open in each group, and nothing requires us to put either of our remaining elements—q and s—in either space. So we put in placeholders that indicate this fact.

Now we work on scenario two: G in one and D in two. With G in one, s has to go in two. As before, we have to keep k and l separate, which we can indicate with placeholders again. Now the remaining element, q, has to go in the lone remaining open spot—in case one. Here's the full diagram of our two scenarios:

	1	2	w
i.	D $^{q}/_{s}$ $^{k}/_{l}$	G $^{s}/_{q}$ $^{l}/_{k}$	A B
ii.	G q $^{k}/_{l}$	D $^{l}/_{k}$ s	A B

Now all we have to do is count. In the first scenario we have two choices of where to put k and l, and for each of these choices we have two choices of where to put q and s, for a total of four possibilities. In the second scenario we have two choices of where to put k and l, and that's it. That gives us a grand total of six possibilities, which is **(D), the credited response**.

SAMPLE GAME THREE: SPATIAL ARRANGEMENT

Although basic ordering and grouping games allow us to make a table and build down as we make new examples, not all games can be diagrammed and worked this way. One of the most common cases where a different approach is needed is a game that requires us to arrange or assign elements in a spatial arrangement—that is, a diagram where some slots are beside one another and some slots are above or below one another.

Fortunately, in a spatial game the board is usually pretty easy to determine. What we want is a "picture" of the layout into which we're putting our elements. This game describes a square array of three rows by three columns, so you'll want to use something that looks like a tic-tac-toe board for your diagram.

On games like these, organization is much more difficult than it is in the games we've seen so far. Before, when we could use a table, we simply set aside the top line for everything we deduced and for clues that could easily be symbolized there. On spatial arrangement games, we need an entire top-line diagram, which is best located somewhere near the top of the page, to contain all the key items of information. Then, as we work new examples, we'll need to redraw a skeletal version of the diagram elsewhere on the page to do our work. In redrawing, we don't have to reproduce all the information from our **top-line diagram**—things like the numbering of spaces, or elements that can't go in particular places, can usually be omitted from your copies, since all of that information is available at the top of the page for your easy reference.

We've got two quick words about redrawing. Some people like to make very involved, detailed copies of their top-line diagram as they go. Although this may make you feel more secure, it should be avoided if at all possible. Most spatial diagrams can be reproduced sufficiently in a few pencil strokes, and the less time you spend making your copy, the more time you'll have to work the question. Also, some test-takers try to get around redrawing by simply making one big copy of the diagram and then erasing for each question. Not only does this eradicate the prior work we found so valuable in our last example, but it also lessens efficiency by forcing you to pick out your deductions from your work on the question every time. This opens up substantial possibilities for confusion, which can lead to wrong answers. The best approach here is to make new copies for each question, keep them simple and small, and do the best you can with the space provided.

Aside from this new wrinkle in working with your diagram, all the clues and concepts in this game should be familiar to you by now. Have fun!

The nine cars participating in a circuit race are arranged in a starting grid that consists of three rows of three cars each. The cars in the first row, listed from the inside of the track to the outside, are numbered 1, 2, and 3; those in the second row are numbered 4, 5, and 6 in the same order; and those in the third row are numbered 7, 8, and 9 in the same order. Thus, the inside column of cars consists of those numbered 1, 4, and 7, listing from the first to third rows; the middle column consists of cars 2, 5, and 8 from first to third; and the outside column consists of cars 3, 6, and 9, again from first to third. Each car is painted a single solid color—green, orange, red, or yellow—and at least one car in the starting grid is painted each of these colors. The assignment of colors to cars in the starting grid is subject to the following conditions:

No two cars in the same row or column are the same color.

Every red car is positioned immediately next to an orange car in the same row.

Car 5 is green.

Car 1 is orange.

1. Which one of the following must be true?

    (A) Car 2 is red.

    (B) Car 3 is yellow.

    (C) Car 4 is yellow.

    (D) Car 6 is green.

    (E) Car 8 is red.

2. Which one of the following could be true?

    (A) Car 2 is green.

    (B) Car 3 is red.

    (C) Car 4 is red.

    (D) Car 7 is green.

    (E) Car 8 is yellow.

3. Which one of the following could be false?

    (A) At least two of the cars are yellow.

    (B) At least two of the cars are green.

    (C) At most two of the cars are red.

    (D) Exactly three of the cars are orange.

    (E) There are at least as many green cars as red cars.

4. If car 7 is the only red car, then which one of the following must be true?

    (A) Car 3 is yellow.

    (B) Car 6 is yellow.

    (C) Car 9 is green.

    (D) Car 9 is orange.

    (E) Car 9 is yellow.

5. If the starting grid includes at least one red car that is in the same column as a green car, then which one of the following could be true?

(A) Car 2 is red and car 3 is green.

(B) Car 2 is red and car 7 is yellow.

(C) Car 2 is yellow and car 7 is red.

(D) Car 3 is yellow and car 8 is red.

(E) Car 3 is green and car 9 is orange.

6. Which one of the following must be true?

(A) Car 3 is green.

(B) Car 7 is green.

(C) Car 8 is orange.

(D) Car 9 is orange.

(E) Car 9 is red.

ANSWERS

1. (C)

2. (D)

3. (A)

4. (E)

5. (A)

6. (C)

EXPLANATIONS

Set Up

As is usual in a spatial arrangement game, the text describes pretty extensively how you should arrange your diagram. The one thing that's slightly unfamiliar in this game is your inventory and the bookkeeping rules surrounding it. Aside from the requirement that each color be used, this game offers no specific restrictions on the number of times each must be. So in this case, our inventory is a list of options, and clearly we'll be reusing some of the colors in filling in our diagram. Here's what it looks like:

Symbolize

Clue 1: This clue is what we called a ground rule earlier. It applies to every element in every portion of the diagram. As such, it's difficult to make a symbol that covers all the possible arrangements forbidden by this clue. The good news is that although clues like this one are difficult to symbolize, they're also difficult to forget. It basically tells you how to operate your diagram: make sure no color is repeated in any column or any row. A decent symbol, using an "x" to stand for any color, would be:

Clue 2: Be careful with this. Although it's tempting to symbolize this clue as a block, it isn't quite one. By this clue, it's perfectly fine to have an o by itself; it's only when we have an r in any given place that an o has to go next to it. This is a kind of one-sided relationship we've seen before. You guessed it; this is actually a conditional clue.

The question of what to do with this clue's contrapositive is an interesting one. Clearly you could flip the order of the symbols around the arrow, put slashes through both, and have a symbol that represents its contrapositive, but it wouldn't be tremendously helpful. In fact, it's virtually impossible to interpret as a symbol. The problem isn't that this conditional clue doesn't have a contrapositive—it most certainly does have one—but instead that the contrapositive is somewhat complicated. Whenever a clue like this leads you to a **complicated contrapositive**, it always pays to spend an extra moment trying to discover in what circumstances you'll actually be able to use it.

In this case, for instance, we know that the contrapositive will apply in any case where it's *not* possible to make a block with o and r next to each other. The consequence will be "not r"—namely, that r *cannot* be put in a particular space. One example of a time we could use this contrapositive is when we're dealing with a space at the end of a row and the single space beside it is occupied by something other than o. In that instance, we wouldn't be able to put an r at the end of the row because doing so would force a violation of the clue. Keep an eye out for spaces like these as we go through the game.

Clues 3 and 4: Here are items of information you can put straight into your top-line diagram and reproduce for each copy you make.

Don't forget to double-check your symbols.

Deduce

Deductions are very important for this game. As we mentioned in the initial description of step 3, ground rules are always good places to look for deductions when a game has them. Here, if we combine clue 1 with the information that car 5 is g, we can immediately deduce that 2, 4, 6, and 8 are all not g. Similarly, the fact that 1 is o tells us that 2, 3, 4, and 7 are all not o.

Here's where the contrapositive of clue 2 really shines. Take a look at slot 4. We know this can't be r because the only space immediately next to it in the same row isn't o. So now we're sure that 4 isn't r, o, or g, but there are only four possible choices of colors! That means 4, for certain, has to be y. Using our ground rule on this new item of information, we know additionally that 1, 6, and 7 are all not y.

Try the contrapositive of clue 2 again, this time on slot 6. Again we have a situation where it's impossible to put o next to it, so the slot cannot be occupied by r. Now we know that 6 can't be r, y, or g; it has to be o! Again, using the ground rule, we can eliminate o as a possibility from slot 9; we already knew that 3 couldn't be o.

We've got all the major deductions that are reasonable to find at this stage, but there are minor deductions that are helpful, if not so crucial. Look at the contrapositive of clue 2 in relation to slot number 3. While we don't know what color 2 is, we do know for certain that it can't be o. This means there's no way to put an o next to 3, which means 3 can't be r. Similar reasoning shows that 8 can't be r either.

Here's a diagram summarizing the deductions we've made so far.

o ¹	g̸ ² g̸	g̸ ³ r̸
y ⁴	g ⁵	o ⁶
g̸ ⁷ y̸	g̸ ⁸ r̸	g̸ ⁹

Since you've already worked the game and checked your answers, in all likelihood you already know that there's another deduction we haven't listed in our diagram above: 8 has to be o. But this is a result of the fact that 8 can't be y, which is not at all clear from the given clues. This is a hidden deduction—one that turns out to be true for some rather indirect reasons—and if you're using a good approach, you should in fact *not* find hidden deductions at this stage of the game. Remember that the point of this step is not to try things at random; after all, what makes 8 a more likely spot for such a deduction than 2, or 7? The fact that you have to stumble across some deductions is a somewhat annoying but inevitable fact of life on LSAT games. The good news is that even if you are working without a deduction, a steady and persistent approach will still get you the answers to the questions. And once you do stumble across a new deduction, you can confirm it and then use it in the rest of the questions in that game.

1. **Which must be true?** This is likely to be a deduction in a game that has so many of them. This might be a question to glance at before moving on, although it's certainly fine to leave it for a second pass as well. If you do glance through the answer choices, you'll see that **(C), the credited response**, is indeed one of our deductions. Although it is possible to do a question like this one using process of elimination, it is time-consuming and should only be a last resort.

2. **Which could be true?** This is a very good second-pass question. (A), (B), and (C) clearly contradict deductions we've made, so we can eliminate them out of hand. If you happen to have generated the example below when you worked question 5, you're done! It shows a case where **(D), the credited response**, is true. Even if you didn't generate this one, however, this question is pretty quick, and you get a nice bonus if you happen to try (E).

   (A) As mentioned above, this contradicts a deduction. This would put two g's in the middle column.

   (B) As mentioned above, this contradicts a deduction. If we try this, we'll see that there's no way to follow rule 2 for this particular red car.

   (C) As mentioned above, this contradicts a deduction. We've known from the start that 4 has to be y.

   (D) **This is the credited response**. As mentioned before, we made this example in working question 5:

o ^{1}	r ^{2}	g ^{3}
y ^{4}	g ^{5}	o ^{6}
g ^{7}	o ^{8}	r ^{9}

(E) This can't happen, and the fact that it can't is useful. If we try y in 8, then look at 7: we have o and y in the same column and y in the same row. But by the contrapositive of clue 2, we can't put an r here either. So 7 must be g. Now look at 9: we have g and y in the same row and o in the same column. The only choice left for this spot is r, but we know that putting r here would violate rule 2! So not only can't 8 be y, but we've already deduced that it can't be g or r either. That means 8 must be o, which is a handy deduction to have if you happen to come across it.

3. **Which could be false?** This is another second-pass question. Given the nature of the answer choices, it's essential to use your prior work as a source of information. The question asks us to find what could be false, which means our answer is something that isn't necessarily true, whereas the other four have to be true all the time.

We certainly have an example from working question 4. Unfortunately, most of our answer choices are true for question 5. If you're lucky enough to have generated the same example as the one we generated for choice (A) in question 5, you'll get the credited response right away. Otherwise, we have to move to process of elimination on the answer choices.

On the LSAT, the only way to evaluate whether a choice has to be true is to try to find a legal example in which it is *false*. So we're trying to generate examples in which each of our choices is not true.

(A) **This is the credited response.** Since we've already deduced that 4 needs to be y, the only way we can make this false is to fill in the remaining spots in our diagram without using another y. If we add the fact that each of our remaining spaces can't be y, we see that 2 must be r, 3 must be g, and 8 must be o (if we didn't know this already). With our new elements added, we see now that 9 must be r, which leaves 7's only possibility as g. Here's the example, which follows all the rules by using only one y:

o [1]	r [2]	g [3]
y [4]	g [5]	o [6]
g [7]	o [8]	r [9]

(B) This has to be true. We're told from the start that 5 is g, so to make this choice false we have to fill in our entire diagram without using another g. If we add the fact that all our open spots aren't g, we see that 7 has to be r, which makes 8 o (again, if we haven't found this as a deduction earlier), so the only choice left for 9 has to be y. But then 3 can't be r, o, g, or y! This can't work.

(C) This one's relatively easy to eliminate. The only way to make this false would be to use 3 r's, but we already have the second row full, and it doesn't include an r. We can't make this one false.

(D) Our initial rules and deductions already include two o's, so the only way we could make this choice false is to use no more o's in making a legal example. If you add this fact and look at the third row, you can see the problem. Once we add the fact that they can't be o, we realize that 7, 8, and 9 also can't be r—otherwise, you'd be violating rule 2. So there's only one possibility left for 8 (that would be y) and only one for 7 (it must be a g). Look at spot 9; now that we've added g and y to the bottom row, we realize there's no color possibility for this spot. We have to use 3 o's (and, additionally, the third has to be in 8).

(E) This one's hard to falsify on its own, but in conjunction with previous choices, it's easy to see that this has to be true. We have to have at least 2 g's—choice (B)—and we have to have at most 2 r's—choice (C). So there's no possible way we could have more r's than g's.

4. **If 7 contains the only r, which must be true?** Not only does this question fill in a spot for us, but it reduces the choices for the other spots to three. If 7 is r, then 8 must be o (clue 2). Look at 2: now we have o in the same row and g and o in the same column; the only remaining color we can choose is y. Look at 3: we have o and y in the same row and o in the same column; the only remaining color we can choose is g. Look at 9: we have r and o in the same row and g and o in the same column; the only remaining color we can choose is y. We've filled in the diagram completely! Here it is:

o ^{1}	y ^{2}	g ^{3}
y ^{4}	g ^{5}	o ^{6}
r ^{7}	o ^{8}	y ^{9}

The only choice that's consistent with our diagram is **(E), the credited response**.

5. **If we have at least one r in the same column as a g, which could be true?**
Although we should begin this question by trying to deduce what we can, we immediately run into a problem: there seem to be very many ways an r could conceivably be in the same column as a g. In cases like these—especially on a "could be true" question—we know by now to go directly to the choices.

    (A) **This is the credited response**, fortunately. Here's one of several ways in which it could be done:

o ¹	r ²	g ³
y ⁴	g ⁵	o ⁶
g ⁷	o ⁸	r ⁹

    (B) This choice violates rule 1 by putting two y's on the inside column.

    (C) If we try this, then 8 must be o to satisfy rule 2. But we still haven't satisfied the condition in the question, so we have to find some way of putting an r and a g in the same column. The only possible place to do this is the outside column, but trying to put the r in 3 will violate clue 2 (there can be no o next to it in the same row), and trying to put the r in 9 will violate clue 1 (by having two r's in the third row).

    (D) This contradicts one of our deductions: that 8 can't be r.

    (E) Making 9 o would contradict rule 1.

6. **Which must be true?** As with all questions like this, we hope that the right answer on this one is a deduction. As it turns out, however, this question asks about the game's hidden deduction—one that you can't expect to find until you've worked through some examples. Most likely, you'll be working this question from the choices.

    As mentioned in question 3, the only way to determine whether an answer choice must be true is to look for a legal example in which it is *false*—that is, you can only eliminate choices on a question like this; you can't verify the right answer directly. We already know from our deductions that choice (D) always has to be false, so we can eliminate that one easily.

The next place to look on a question like this one is your prior work—again, you're looking for legal examples where the answer choice is not true. At the very least you have your example from question 4. In that one, 7 is r and 9 is y, so that allows us to eliminate (B) and (E) immediately. (A) and (C) are the only choices left. If you happen to have generated a legal example where 3 is y, then you can eliminate answer choice (A) and get immediately to the credited response. Otherwise, you have to do it by hand.

(A) This choice doesn't have to be true—it's possible for 3 to be y. Here's an example:

o ^{1}	r ^{2}	y ^{3}
y ^{4}	g ^{5}	o ^{6}
r ^{7}	o ^{8}	g ^{9}

(B) As mentioned above, we've made an example before where this is false. Our example in (A) also shows this does not have to be true.

(C) **This is the credited response.** Making 8 y—the only other conceivable choice given our deductions—forces 7 to be g. Then 9 cannot be r, o, g, or y. This choice must be true.

(D) As mentioned above, this choice actually contradicts one of our deductions. It can't be true.

(E) As mentioned above, we've made an example before where this is false. Our example in (A) also shows this does not have to be true.

SUGGESTIONS FOR FURTHER PREPARATION

After going through just these three examples, you've probably gotten the idea that practice and familiarity are incredibly important for performing your best on the Games section on test day. The Logical Reasoning sections and even the Reading Comprehension section similarly require a degree of familiarity for you to achieve the highest possible score.

Fortunately, LSAC is unusual among organizations that make standardized tests in that they are quite willing to disclose the tests and questions they give. The scored sections of the majority of LSAT exams are available for purchase from LSAC, through their website or by phone or mail. There is no better source of practice than the actual exams themselves, and there are literally dozens to choose from. Make good use of them.

Although this treatment of the games section is thorough when it comes to fundamental approaches and ideas, there is a lot more to learn. The Princeton Review's *Cracking the LSAT* goes through the concepts mentioned here in greater detail, and moves on to things like in/out games, distribution deductions, and the theory and construction of the most difficult games. Additional practice is essential, but further instruction—whether through The Princeton Review's books, courses, or tutoring or through some other outlet—can be incredibly helpful in making the most of that practice. Whatever method you choose, be sure to make a plan for solid preparation and stick to it. Good luck!

ABOUT THE AUTHOR

Eric Owens, Esq., lives in Chicago with his brilliant, lovely, and forgiving wife, Rachel Brown. He recently left private practice to try to convince the Foreign Service that he would make a worthwhile diplomat. It's a slow process. He is an SAT teacher, tutor, and master trainer and a GMAT teacher and tutor for The Princeton Review.

NOTES

NOTES

Graduate School Entrance Tests

Business School

Is an MBA in your future? If so, you'll need to take the GMAT. The GMAT is a computer-based test offered year round, on most days of the week. October and November are the most popular months for testing appointments. Most business schools require you to have a few years of work experience before you apply, but that doesn't mean you should put off taking the GMAT. Scores are valid for up to five years, so you should take the test while you're still in college and in the test-taking frame of mind.

Law School

If you want to be able to call yourself an "esquire", you'll need to take the LSAT. Most students take the LSAT in the fall of their senior year—either the October or the December administration. The test is also offered in February and in June. The June test is the only afternoon administration – so if your brain doesn't start functioning until the P.M., this might be the one for you. Just make sure to take it in June of your junior year if you want to meet the application deadlines.

Medical School

The MCAT is offered twice each year, in April and in August. It's a beastly eight-hour exam, but it's a necessary evil if you want to become a doctor. Since you'll need to be familiar with the physics, chemistry, and biology tested on the exam, you'll probably want to wait until April of your junior year to take the test— that's when most students take the MCAT. If you wait until August to give it a shot, you'll still be able to meet application deadlines, but you won't have time to take it again if you're not satisfied with your results.

Other Graduate and Ph.D. Programs

For any other graduate or Ph.D. program, be it art history or biochemical engineering, you'll need to take the GRE General Test. This is another computer-based test, and, like the GMAT, it's offered year-round on most days of the week. The most popular test dates are in late summer and in the fall. Take the test no later than October or November before you plan to enter graduate school to ensure that you meet all application deadlines (and the all-important financial aid deadlines) and to leave yourself some room to take it again if you're not satisfied with your scores.

Understanding the Tests

MCAT

Structure and Format

The Medical College Admission Test (MCAT) is a six-hour paper-and-pencil exam that can take up to eight or nine hours to administer.

The MCAT consists of four scored sections that always appear in the same order:

1. Physical Sciences: 100 minutes; 77 physics and general chemistry questions

2. Verbal Reasoning: 85 minutes; 60 questions based on nine passages

3. Writing Sample: two 30-minute essays

4. Biological Sciences: 100 minutes; 77 biology and organic chemistry questions

Scoring

The Physical Sciences, Biological Sciences, and Verbal Reasoning sections are each scored on a scale of 1 to 15, with 8 as the average score. These scores will be added together to form your Total Score. The Writing Sample is scored from J (lowest) to T (highest), with O as the average score.

Test Dates

The MCAT is offered twice each year—in April and August.

Registration

The MCAT is administered and scored by the MCAT Program Office under the direction of the AAMC. To request a registration packet, you can write to the MCAT Program Office, P.O. Box 4056, Iowa City, Iowa 52243 or call 319-337-1357.

GRE

Structure and Format

The Graduate Record Examinations (GRE) General Test is a multiple-choice test for applicants to graduate school that is taken on computer. It is a computer-adaptive test (CAT), consisting of three sections.

- One 30-minute, 30-question "Verbal Ability" (vocabulary and reading) section

- One 45-minute, 28-question "Quantitative Ability" (math) section

- An Analytical Writing Assessment, consisting of two essay tasks

  o One 45-minute "Analysis of an Issue" task

  o One 30-minute "Analysis of an Argument" task

The GRE is a computer-adaptive test, which means that it uses your performance on previous questions to determine which question you will be asked next. The software calculates your score based on the number of questions you answer correctly, the difficulty of the questions you answer, and the number of questions you complete. Questions that appear early in the test impact your score to a greater degree than do those that come toward the end of the exam.

Scoring

You will receive a Verbal score and a Math score, each ranging from 200 to 800, as well as an Analytic Writing Assessment (AWA) score ranging from 0 to 6.

Test Dates

The GRE is offered year-round in testing centers, by appointment.

Registration

To register for the GRE, call 1-800-GRE-CALL or register online at www.GRE.org.

Understanding the Tests

LSAT

Structure and Format

The Law School Admission Test (LSAT) is a four-hour exam comprised of five 35-minute multiple-choice test sections of approximately 25 questions each, plus an essay:

- Reading Comprehension (1 section)
- Analytical Reasoning (1 section)
- Logical Reasoning (2 sections)
- Experimental Section (1 section)

Scoring

- Four of the five multiple-choice sections count toward your final LSAT score
- The fifth multiple-choice section is an experimental section used solely to test new questions for future exams
- Correct responses count equally and no points are deducted for incorrect or blank responses
- Test takers get a final, scaled score between 120 and 180
- The essay is not scored, and is rarely used to evaluate your candidacy by admissions officers

Test Dates

The LSAT is offered four times each year— in February, June, October, and December.

Registration

To register for the LSAT, visit www.LSAC.org to order a registration book or to register online.

GMAT

Structure and Format

The Graduate Management Admission Test (GMAT) is a multiple-choice test for applicants to business school that is taken on computer. It is a computer-adaptive test (CAT), consisting of three sections:

- Two 30-minute essays to be written on the computer: Analysis of an Argument and Analysis of an Issue
- One 75-minute, 37-question Math section: Problem Solving and Data Sufficiency
- One 75-minute, 41-question Verbal section: Sentence Corrections, Critical Reasoning, and Reading Comprehension

The GMAT is a computer-adaptive test, which means that it uses your performance on previous questions to determine which question you will be asked next. The software calculates your score based on the number of questions you answer correctly, the difficulty of the questions you answer, and the number of questions you complete. Questions that appear early in the test impact your score to a greater degree than do those that come toward the end of the exam.

Scoring

You will receive a composite score ranging from 200 to 800 in 10-point increments, in addition to a Verbal score and a Math score, each ranging from 0 to 60. You will also receive an Analytic Writing Assessment (AWA) score ranging from 0 to 6.

Test Dates

The GMAT is offered year-round in testing centers, by appointment.

Registration

To register for the GMAT, call 1-800-GMAT-NOW or register online at www.MBA.com.

Dispelling the Myths about Test Preparation and Admissions

MYTH: If you have a solid GPA, your test score isn't as important for getting into a college or graduate school.

FACT: While it is true that admissions committees consider several factors in their admissions decisions, including test scores, GPA, work or extra-curricular experience, and letters of recommendation, it is not always true that committees will overlook your test scores if you are strong in other areas. Particularly for large programs with many applicants, standardized tests are often the first factor that admissions committees use to evaluate prospective students.

MYTH: Standardized exams test your basic skills or innate ability; therefore your score cannot be significantly improved through studying.

FACT: Nothing could be farther from the truth. You can benefit tremendously from exposure to actual tests and expert insight into the test writers' habits and the most commonly used tricks.

MYTH: There are lots of skills you can learn to help you improve your math score, but you can't really improve your verbal score.

FACT: The single best way to improve your verbal score is to improve your vocabulary. Question types in the verbal reasoning sections of standardized tests all rely upon your understanding of the words in the questions and answer choices. If you know what the words mean, you'll be able to answer the questions quickly and accurately. Improving your critical reading skills is also very important.

MYTH: Standardized exams measure your intelligence.

FACT: While test scores definitely matter, they do NOT test your intelligence. The scores you achieve reflect only how prepared you were to take that particular exam and how good a test taker you are.

Hyperlearning *MCAT Prep Course*

The Princeton Review Difference

Nearly 40% of all MCAT test takers take the exam twice due to inadequate preparation the first time. **Do not be one of them.**

Our Approach to Mastering the MCAT

You will need to conquer both the verbal and the science portions of the MCAT to get your best score. But it might surprise you to learn that the Verbal Reasoning and Writing Sample are the most important sub-sections on the test. That is why we dedicate twice as much class time to these sections as does any other national course! We will help you to develop superlative reading and writing skills so you will be ready to write well crafted, concise essay responses. And of course, we will also help you to develop a thorough understanding of the basic science concepts and problem-solving techniques that you will need to ace the MCAT.

Total Preparation: 41 Class Sessions

With 41 class sessions, our MCAT course ensures that you will be prepared and confident by the time you take the test.

The Most Practice Materials

You will receive more than 3,000 pages of practice materials and 1,300 pages of supplemental materials, and all are yours to keep. Rest assured that our material is always fresh. Each year we write a new set of practice passages to reflect the style and content of the most recent tests. You will also take five full-length practice MCATs under actual testing conditions, so you can build your test-taking stamina and get used to the time constraints.

Specialist Instructors

Your course will be led by a team of between two and five instructors—each an expert in his or her specific subjects. Our instructors are carefully screened and undergo a rigorous national training program. In fact, the quality of our instructors is a major reason students recommend our course to their friends.

Get the Score You Want

We guarantee you will be completely satisfied with your MCAT score!* Our students boast an average MCAT score improvement of ten points.**

*If you attend all class sessions, complete all tests and homework, finish the entire course, take the MCAT at the next administration and do not void your test, and you still are not satisfied with your score, we will work with you again at no additional cost for one of the next two MCAT administrations.
**Independently verified by International Communications Research.

ClassSize-8 *Classroom Courses for the GRE, LSAT, and GMAT*

Small Classes

We know students learn better in smaller classes. With no more than eight students in a Princeton Review class, your instructor knows who you are, and works closely with you to identify your strengths and weaknesses. You will be as prepared as possible. When it comes to your future, you shouldn't be lost in a crowd of students.

Guaranteed Satisfaction

A prep course is a big investment—in terms of both time and money. At The Princeton Review, your investment will pay off. Our LSAT students improve by an average of 7 points, our GRE students improve by an average of 212 points, and our GMAT students boast an average score improvement of 92.5 points—the best score improvement in the industry.* We guarantee that you will be satisfied with your results. If you're not, we'll work with you again for free.**

Expert Instructors

Princeton Review instructors are energetic and smart—they've all scored in the 95th percentile or higher on standardized tests. Our instructors will make your experience engaging and effective.

Free Extra Help

We want you to get your best possible score on the test. If you need extra help on a particular topic, your instructor is happy to meet with you outside of class to make sure you are comfortable with the material—at no extra charge!

Online Lessons, Tests, and Drills

Princeton Review *ClassSize-8* Courses are the only classroom courses that have online lessons designed to support each class session. You can practice concepts you learn in class, spend some extra time on topics that you find challenging, or prepare for an upcoming class. And you'll have access as soon as you enroll, so you can get a head start on your test preparation.

The Most Comprehensive, Up-to-Date Materials

Our research and development team studies the tests year-round to stay on top of trends and to make sure you learn what you need to get your best score.

*Independently verified by International Communications Research (ICR).

**Some restrictions apply.

Online *and* LiveOnline *Courses* for the GRE, LSAT, and GMAT

The Best of Both Worlds

We've combined our high-quality, compre hensive test preparation with a convenient, multimedia format that works around your schedule and your needs.

Online *and* LiveOnline *Courses*

Lively, Engaging Lessons

If you think taking an online course means staring at a screen and struggling to pay attention, think again. Our lessons are engaging and interactive – you'll never just read blocks of text or passively watch video clips. Princeton Review online courses feature animation, audio, interactive lessons, and self-directed navigation.

Customized, Focused Practice

The course software will discover your personal strengths and weaknesses. It will help you to prioritize and focus on the areas that are most important to your success. Of course, you'll have access to dozens of hours' worth of lessons and drills covering all areas of the test, so you can practice as much or as little as you choose.

Help at your Fingertips

Even though you'll be working on your own, you won't be left to fend for yourself. We're ready to help at any time of the day or night: you can chat online with a live Coach, check our Frequently Asked Questions database, or talk to other students in our discussion groups.

LiveOnline *Course*

Extra Features

In addition to self-directed online lessons, practice tests, drills, and more, you'll partici- pate in five live class sessions and three extra help sessions given in real time over the Internet. You'll get the live interaction of a classroom course from the comfort of your own home.

ExpressOnline *Course*

The Best in Quick Prep

If your test is less than a month away, or you just want an introduction to our legendary strategies, this mini-course may be the right choice for you. Our multimedia lessons will walk you through basic test- taking strategies to give you the edge you need on test day.

1-2-1 Private Tutoring

The Ultimate in Personalized Attention

If you're too busy for a classroom course, prefer learning at your kitchen table, or simply want your instructor's undivided attention,
1-2-1 Private Tutoring may be for you.

Focused on You

In larger classrooms, there is always one student who monopolizes the instructor's attention. With *1-2-1* Private Tutoring, that student is you. Your instructor will tailor the course to your needs – greater focus on the subjects that cause you trouble, and less focus on the subjects that you're comfortable with. You can get all the instruction you need in less time than you would spend in a class.

Expert Tutors

Our outstanding tutoring staff is comprised of specially selected, rigorously trained instructors who have performed exceptionally in the classroom. They have scored in the top percentiles on standardized tests and received the highest student evaluations.

Schedules to Meet Your Needs

We know you are busy, and preparing for the test is perhaps the last thing you want to do in your "spare" time. The Princeton Review *1-2-1* Private Tutoring Program will work around your schedule.

Additional Online Lessons and Resources

The learning continues outside of your tutoring sessions. Within the Online Student Center*, you will have access to math, verbal, AWA, and general strategy lessons to supplement your private instruction. Best of all, they are accessible to you 24 hours a day,
7 days a week.

*Available for LSAT, GRE, and GMAT

www.PrincetonReview.com

The Princeton Review Admissions Services

At The Princeton Review, we care about your ability to get accepted to the best school for you. But, we all know getting accepting involves much more than just doing well on standardized tests. That's why, in addition to our test preparation services, we also offer free admissions services to students looking to enter college or graduate school. You can find these services on our website, *www.PrincetonReview.com*, the best online resource for researching, applying to, and learning how to pay for the right school for you.

No matter what type of program you're applying to—undergraduate, graduate, law, business, or medical—**PrincetonReview.com has the free tools, services, and advice you need to navigate the admissions process.** Read on to learn more about the services we offer.

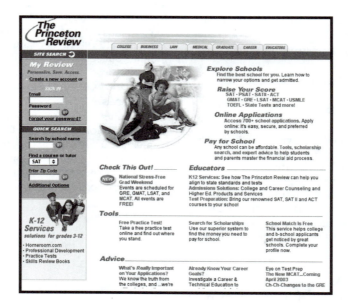

Research Schools
www.PrincetonReview.com/Research

PrincetonReview.com features an interactive tool called **Advanced School Search.** When you use this tool, you enter stats and information about yourself to find a list of schools that fit your needs. From there you can read statistical and editorial information about every accredited business school, law school, medical school, and graduate school.

If you are applying to business school, make sure to use **School Match.** You tell us your scores, interests, and preferences and Princeton Review partner schools will contact you.

No matter what type of school or specialized program you are considering, **PrincetonReview.com has free articles and advice, in addition to our tools, to help you make the right choice.**

Apply to School
www.PrincetonReview.com/Apply

For most students, completing the school application is the most stressful part of the admissions process. PrincetonReview.com's powerful **Online School Application Engine** makes it easy to apply.

Paper applications are mostly a thing of the past. And, our hundreds of partner schools tell us they prefer to receive your applications online.

Using our online application service is simple:

- Enter information once and the common data automatically transfers onto each application.
- Save your applications and access them at any time to edit and perfect.
- Submit electronically or print and mail in.
- Pay your application fee online, using an e-check, or mail the school a check.

Our powerful application engine is built to accommodate all your needs.

Pay for School
www.PrincetonReview.com/Finance

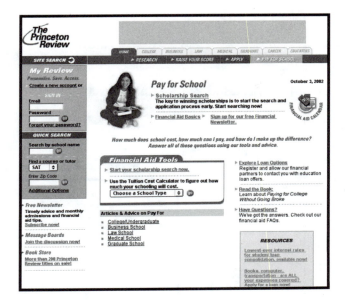

The financial aid process is confusing for everyone. But don't worry. Our free online tools, services, and advice can help you plan for the future and get the money you need to pay for school.

Our **Scholarship Search** engine will help you find free money, although often scholarships alone won't cover the cost of high tuitions. So, we offer other tools and resources to help you navigate the entire process.

Filling out the FAFSA and CSS Profile can be a daunting process, use our **Strategies for both forms** to make sure you answer the questions correctly the first time.

If scholarships and government aid aren't enough to swing the cost of tuition, we'll help you secure student loans. The Princeton Review has partnered with a select group of reputable financial institutions who will help **explore all your loans options**.

If you know how to work the financial aid process, you'll learn you don't have to **eliminate a school based on tuition.**

Be a Part of the PrincetonReview.com Community

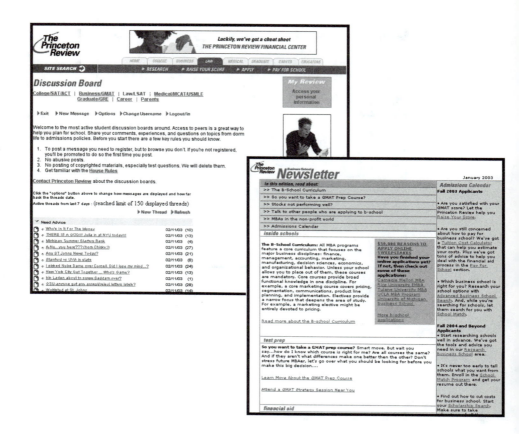

PrincetonReview.com's **Discussion Boards** and **Free Newsletters** are additional services to help you to get information about the admissions process from your peers and from The Princeton Review experts.

Book Store
www.PrincetonReview.com/college/
Bookstore.asp

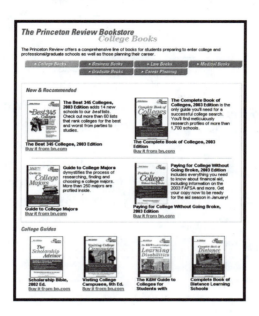

In addition to this book, we publish hundreds of other titles, including guidebooks that highlight life on campus, student opinion, and all the statistical data that you need to know about any school you are considering. Just a few of the titles that we offer are:

- Complete Book of Business Schools
- Complete Book of Law Schools
- Complete Book of Medical Schools
- The Best 351 Colleges
- The K&W Guide to Colleges for Students with Learning Disabilities or Attention Deficit Disorder
- Guide to College Majors
- Paying for College Without Going Broke

For a complete listing of all of our titles, visit our **online book store**:

www.princetonreview.com/college/bookstore.asp